THE NORTHWEST GARDEN MANIFESTO

THE NORTHWEST GARDEN MANIFESTO

CREATE, RESTORE, AND MAINTAIN A SUSTAINABLE YARD

JOHN J. ALBERS, PhD

PHOTOGRAPHY BY DAVID E. PERRY

SKIPSTONE

Published by Skipstone, an imprint of Mountaineers Books
Printed in China
21 20 19 18   1 2 3 4 5

Design: Jen Grable
Cover photograph by David E. Perry
All photographs by David E. Perry
Page 2: *Urban gardens can be both beautiful and sustainable.*
Page 224: *This courtyard garden is an inspiration.*

Library of Congress Cataloging-in-Publication Data
Names: Albers, John J., author. | Perry, David E., photographer.
Title: The Northwest garden manifesto : create, restore, and maintain a
   sustainable yard / John J. Albers, PhD ; photography by David E. Perry.
Description: Seattle, Washington : Skipstone, [2018] | Includes
   bibliographical references and index.
Identifiers: LCCN 2017018881 (print) | LCCN 2017022148 (ebook) |
   ISBN 9781680511109 (e-book) | ISBN 9781680511093 (pbk.)
Subjects: LCSH: Gardening--Northwest, Pacific.
Classification: LCC SB453.2.N83 (ebook) | LCC SB453.2.N83 A43 2018 (print) |
   DDC 635.09795--dc23
LC record available at https://lccn.loc.gov/2017018881

ISBN (paperback): 978-1-68051-109-3
ISBN (ebook): 978-1-68051-110-9

Printed on FSC®-certified paper

Skipstone books may be purchased for corporate, educational, or other promotional sales, and our authors are available for a wide range of events. For information on special discounts or booking an author, contact our customer service at 800-553-4453 or mbooks@mountaineersbooks.org.

Skipstone
1001 SW Klickitat Way
Suite 201
Seattle, Washington 98134
206.223.6303
www.skipstonebooks.org
www.mountaineersbooks.org

LIVE LIFE. MAKE RIPPLES.

CONTENTS

INTRODUCTION

A MANIFESTO FOR NORTHWEST GARDENS

For millions of years, the earth has teemed with life, everything evolving in an intricate and infinitely complex process. From the very first oxygen-producing microbe to the last dodo to your local favorite *Homo sapiens*, an incredible diversity of life-forms, or *biodiversity*, has called this world home. Today is no different. Yet, as more and more of us humans gather in urban environments, we are seeing a noticeable shift in biodiversity—and not always for the good.

There are many wonderful things about big cities and the variety they attract. Where else can you eat biscuits and gravy for breakfast, dim sum for lunch, and enchiladas for dinner? But, unfortunately, as green spaces are razed to make room for new restaurants or apartment buildings, the original tenants—the plants, animals, insects, and microbes—find themselves out on the street, so to speak. We may not feel the repercussions of these changes immediately, but in the long run we'll find that their loss is our loss too.

The disappearance of plant and animal habitat, the introduction and spread of invasive species, the overexploitation of natural resources, increased pollution, and climate change collectively pose a very real threat to the array of life-forms on Earth and the ability of ecosystems to perform the functions and services that make the planet livable for all of us. If you've read

OPPOSITE: *Growing tomatoes in the city can be easy and satisfying.*

This large native bigleaf maple softens the city's hardscapes and has a calming effect on its inhabitants.

a newspaper or watched the news lately, you're probably well aware that we've got a problem, and that there's no time to stand around waiting for someone else to fix it. We must act now to preserve and restore biodiversity, especially in cities, where the majority of us live and work, to ensure that nature's bounty continues to be available in the future. We must learn how to change the way we think about our limited natural resources, the way we build and maintain our cities, the way we live.

All gardeners who tend the land in cities—from homeowners and community gardeners to park staff and land managers—play a vital role in supporting and improving the health of our ecosystem. Of course, maintaining (or re-creating) happy and healthy urban ecosystems brings a whole host of other benefits, including many positive impacts on health and well-being. Gardening provides a therapeutic break from day-to-day stressors; an energizing respite from the strain of indoor, desk-centered study; a breath of fresh air; and a way to get the blood pumping after a long workweek. Most gardeners will tell you that biting into a freshly picked summer tomato or tart autumn apple that they've cultivated themselves is an entirely different experience from munching on grocery store produce. I could go on and on about the personal

LEFT: *Engaging kids with the outdoors can be simple and fun.* **RIGHT:** *Gardening is often hard work but it brings many rewards.*

benefits of gardening—the beauty, the tranquility, the deep sense of achievement—but of course there's so much more to it than that.

Every city garden has the potential to be not only a singular oasis but also a valuable link to the broader ecosystem. For me, gardening provides a bigger perspective, a wider vision of how I fit into the natural order. Gardening reveals how a healthy backyard directly contributes to the health of the planet. Adding to the world's greenness, be it at home, along a city street, or in a community garden, fosters a strong sense of belonging to the land. And if you can get the kids involved, through environmental education or simply by letting them jump into that irresistible pile of just-raked leaves, then there's a better chance that a fundamental respect for the earth and a call to steward it will carry on to the next generation.

Horticulture, landscaping, and environmental stewardship have been my passion for more than three decades. For the past fifteen years I have had the joy and privilege of creating and living within a four-acre botanical garden. I have given tours of it and presentations to countless gardeners, talking with my community about the sustainable landscape practices that enable Northwest gardens to thrive. I wrote *The Northwest Garden Manifesto* in order to share my interest, expertise, and enthusiasm with a wider audience. Through this book, I hope to show how you too can be involved in developing your own urban garden as well as volunteering to help develop the public green spaces around you, and that this challenge is accessible, gratifying, and fun. We'll work from the ground up, beginning with evaluating your existing yard or green space and then considering practical ways to restore biodiversity, improve the

The author leading a tour of his garden

soil, select and plant the right plants for your space, and use sustainable resources for ongoing maintenance. I'll also show how you can attract beneficial wildlife, including pollinators, and minimize the establishment and spread of invasive species. And I'll demonstrate how all of this ties nicely into the bigger picture: how, through our gardening, we can reduce water overuse and pollution, lower the temperature of urban heat islands, and improve air quality.

With your active participation in the ecological community, you can play a role in the preservation of open space and natural areas, in the forestalling of the destruction of our environment, and in encouraging the recovery of the natural world. As you improve your garden and other urban landscapes, you will be making a substantial contribution to your own well-being and that of your city.

Ultimately, what I am offering is a practical guide, researched in the library, the nursery, the garden store, and, of course, my botanical garden. It's for anyone from novice to expert city-dwelling gardener, but particularly for someone who gardens, likes to garden, and wants to garden in a more sustainable way. I hope *The Northwest Garden Manifesto* will support you in your effort to sustain, protect, and restore urban biodiversity, and to help each of us make a positive and enduring change.

PART 1

GETTING STARTED

WELCOME
TO THE
DANNY WOO
INTERNATIONAL DISTRICT
COMMUNITY GARDENS
The Garden is Closed at Night
NO TRESPASSING
9:00 pm to 6:00 am
Except for Special Events

PLEASE RESPECT
OUR GARDENS DURING
YOUR VISIT

Craig Tosh Shimabukuro
January 9, 1948 – March 16, 2004
• Father   • Children
   Tosh   Ian
• Mother   Ryan
   Esther   Rachel
• Wife
   Wadiyah

喜　和　真　智
LOVE PEACE TRUTH WISDOM

1

NATURE IN THE CITY

If you live in a city, then you live within a particular kind of nature, within many kinds of ecosystems. Urban landscapes are both unique and diverse, with the man-made environment of shopping malls and condominiums and subway stations and all manner of concrete and glass constructions existing alongside the remnants of forest and wetlands, leftover agricultural areas such as grasslands and fields, maintained city parks, and private yards and gardens. Today more than half of the world's population, and more than 80 percent of the people in highly developed countries, lives in urban areas like this.

Yet the ecosystems within cities are rarely healthy and thriving. Unfortunately, the environment and the number of species in it have declined more rapidly in the past sixty years than at any other time in human history. This is because humans have significantly altered approximately half of Earth's land surface, either without understanding the impact of development or ignoring early and ongoing warning signs of the consequences.

Cities are a big source of biodiversity degradation. They not only eat up plant and animal habitat but require large quantities of materials and energy and in turn produce substantial amounts of waste; garbage is just a small part of it. Just as speeding air molecules heat up, all this urban busyness causes higher temperatures, as much as 10°F higher compared with surrounding rural areas, and especially at night—an effect called the *urban heat island*. Blame it on the usual suspects: reduced tree canopies, increased traffic, and the fossil-fuel emissions

OPPOSITE: *Seattle's Danny Woo International District Community Gardens provide a welcoming, green oasis.*

13

LEFT: *Hardscapes in cities have a big impact on the surrounding environment.* **RIGHT:** *Invasive Himalayan blackberry blankets our cities' transportation corridors and vacant lots.*

of industry, which act like insulation by keeping heat from escaping. Plus, dark-colored roofing and paving absorb solar radiation during the day and release it as heat at night. To counter this, people use more energy for air-conditioning and that extra refrigerator in the garage to keep the beer ice-cold, which just spurs the cycle on. Then it rains, and all the pollutants and shed tire rubber run off into nearby streams and rivers, which, as you might imagine, is bad news for all the organisms living in marine habitat.

All of this altered land, disturbed water, and sullied air messes with native nutrient cycles and food webs, creating conditions that are more welcoming to harmful invasive species. Think of the Himalayan blackberry (*Rubus armeniacus*), which, once established, can make it difficult for native species to take hold. Invasive species decrease local diversity and rapidly homogenize landscapes, funda-

mentally changing key natural processes such as nutrient and water cycles and the compositions of plant and animal communities.

The variety of soil organisms in urban soils is often low because these soils differ from undisturbed soils in the way they drain water, as well as in their structural profile and chemical properties. Soils compacted by construction, heavy foot traffic, or parking have less air space for soil organisms and a reduced ability to absorb water. Urban soils are often contaminated by heavy metals and toxic residues. Land previously used for an apple orchard, for example, can contain significant amounts of lead and arsenic from application of pesticides.

This list of the ways cities damage biodiversity is by no means comprehensive, and still it can cause feelings of sadness or anger (at least, it does so in me). But I hope that, rather than causing you despair, it pushes you to act. While not necessarily pristine natural areas, human-modified landscapes can still provide habitat for numerous plants, animals, and other organisms—if they are created with thoughtfulness, foresight, and care.

WHAT IS A HEALTHY ECOSYSTEM?

Before we try to fix all this human-caused environmental degradation, we must first understand what a healthy ecosystem really is. A healthy ecosystem has normal biological and chemical processes, such as climate regulation, soil formation, and generation of food and habitat for animals and plants, is generally free from distress and damage, maintains its organization and autonomy over time, and is resilient to stress. This means that a healthy ecosystem does all the things it's supposed to do while also adapting to climate change and regenerating itself after being disturbed or harmed.

A large number of species is vital to a healthy ecosystem, so that if external stressors kill off one group, another group or groups can take its place and take over its job. High species diversity buffers ecosystems against environmental strains such as pests, diseases, and changes in temperature, which otherwise could cause not only local species loss but also ecosystem disruption. Think of the rain forest on the Olympic Peninsula in Washington State, or Discovery Park in Seattle: Like my own garden, with its urban forest remnant along with a large number of plant species, these are examples of healthy ecosystems. The ecological fabric of these places is made up of all sorts of species and populations, which increase the systems' resiliency in the face of environmental change. Clearly, for sustainability, biodiversity is an absolute requirement.

The Stroll Gallery in Albers Vista Gardens illustrates a species-rich, healthy ecosystem.

ECOLOGY BASICS

Before we go any further, here are some basic concepts you'll need to understand as you read this book.

- **Ecology:** The scientific study of the interaction of organisms with their physical (nonliving) and biological (living) environments.
- **Ecosystem:** An interacting, complex, functional community of plants, animals, and microorganisms living in a particular chemical and physical environment within a defined area.
- **Habitat:** The environment—including the temperature, precipitation, wind, elevation, and other chemical and physical properties—in which animals, plants, and other organisms live.
- **Biodiversity:** The vast variety and full range of life-forms on Earth across all biological levels, from genes to species to populations to communities of organisms in different ecosystems.

WHAT A HEALTHY ECOSYSTEM MEANS TO US: ECOSYSTEM SERVICES

As you sit reading this book, perhaps freshly showered and fed, while birds fly or cars zoom past your window, consider all the ecological goods and services you benefit from. By "goods and services" I mean the wood and metal and rock that make up your shelter, the water and food recently used and consumed, and all that plants do for us. All of these originate in nature's warehouse of goods and services. The 2005 Millennium Ecosystem Assessment (see Resources, at the back of this book) grouped them into four broad categories: *supporting, provisioning, regulating,* and *cultural.* All are necessary for the sustenance and well-being of plants and animals, including humans.

Supporting Services

An example of a *supporting* service that sustains life on Earth is the repeated cycling of a given element through all its different forms and hosts, from the nonliving environment to living organisms and back again. This is known as a *nutrient cycle.* While organic matter is formed through photosynthesis, nutrients are converted into plant tissue through absorption and

A young seedling in a handful of healthy, fertile soil.

Orchards are a perfect example of a provisioning service.

metabolic processes (called *primary production*). The nutrient cycle's most important elements are carbon, hydrogen, oxygen, and nitrogen, which make up more than 95 percent of most living tissue. Other essential elements for normal plant growth include phosphorous, potassium, sulfur, calcium, and magnesium.

The nutrient cycle underpins everything and, as far as we know, has been in equilibrium for millions of years in both terrestrial and marine ecosystems (although human actions may be upsetting this balance). It provides virtually all the energy required by all living organisms and powers all ecological processes.

Provisioning Services

The products we and all other living things obtain from ecosystems come to us through what are called *provisioning* services. Oceans, rivers, streams, and lakes provide us with fish, shellfish, seaweed, and other valuable elements, while terrestrial areas—including both wildernesses and farms, orchards, and gardens—give us fruit, vegetables, meat, dairy goods, and other products. Forests and woodland plants provide many of our medicines, oils, resins, and dyes, as well as wood for fuel, shelter, and many other products.

Regulating Services

Ecosystem processes *regulate* the environment. For example, plants filter the air by trapping atmospheric contaminants and particulates and by binding and detoxifying pollutants on their leaf surfaces. They remove carbon dioxide from the atmosphere and store the carbon in their tissues, and they regulate local climate by shading and facilitating evaporation.

ELEMENTS OF THE URBAN LANDSCAPE

City landscapes exist in myriad forms and provide many kinds of habitat. Each of the common features below is important for wildlife and organisms that call these spaces home.

- *Private home gardens* are often a mix of open and sheltered spaces, plants in containers, and plants in the ground. Having more and varied space allows for creativity—and a diversity of organisms big and small.
- *Planters* are as easy to create as they are versatile. These containers can be added to decks or patios, alleys or parking strips. A small planting area can give refuge to wildlife with limited range requirements, create cover and food for birds and other animals, and provide space for flowers that benefit pollinators.
- *Green roofs* are perfect for those who don't have a lot of ground space, and developers choose to install them because they can moderate heat and stormwater issues. Whether they are drought-tolerant succulents and grasses or kale and cilantro nurtured in rooftop gardens, green roofs can attract a diversity of birds and pollinating insects.
- *Community gardens* bring a variety of people together for a common purpose: to garden and to enjoy the fruits of their labors. For apartment dwellers, or renters who want a stable piece of land no matter where home is, community gardens are perfect for growing fresh food and plants, as well as getting to know the neighbors.
- *Tree canopies* in residential properties, city parks, or woodlands and along city streets provide feeding, nesting, and breeding habitat for a plethora of bird life and invertebrates. The floor of urban woodlands and city parks, with its leaf litter, snags, decaying logs, and groundcovers, provides a shady home for many kinds of organisms.
- *Windbreaks* can reduce heating costs, particularly in regions like Puget Sound, if you live on a bluff or otherwise exposed area where the wind whips up during winter storms. Windbreaks are basically walls made of vegetation, such as a dense row of evergreens and shrubs, planted upwind from a building and at an angle perpendicular to the prevailing winter winds. If well placed, these will not only protect the building from the destructive effects of the elements, but also insulate it and provide a habitat for wildlife.
- *Ponds, lakes, streams, reservoirs, and other urban waterways* serve as habitat for amphibians, invertebrates, and waterfowl.

Freshwater wetlands and estuaries absorb, filter out, and recycle nutrients such as nitrogen and phosphorus as needed; healthy watersheds ensure clean drinking water in our communities. Floodplain ecosystems can help regulate flooding, increasingly important

LEFT: *Salt marshes play a valuable role in the coastal ecosystem.* **RIGHT:** *The outdoors delivers cultural services to us in a variety of ways.*

as our weather becomes more extreme. Tree canopies and shrubs intercept rain and slow its progress to the soil surface, while plant roots bind the soil, both processes helping to reduce erosion. In coastal areas, mangrove forests and salt marshes play a key role in buffering coastal areas from ocean surges from storms. When in balance, an ecosystem has the ability to right itself, come pest or high water.

Cultural Services

Ecosystems have many less obvious, nonmaterial benefits, or *cultural* services: recreation, spiritual enrichment, intellectual development, and aesthetic enjoyment, just to name a few. Humans have been trying to understand the wonders and workings of nature since a stick became a tool. Outdoors, we can bird-watch, hunt, camp, hike, bicycle, ski, snowboard, swim, boat, and fish. Nature is a rich source of inspiration for art, poetry, and

folklore, and a locus for focusing our sense of local identity.

PRESERVING OUR ECOSYSTEM SERVICES

Healthy urban ecosystems generate a wide variety of services, including erosion control, air filtration, water purification, noise reduction, and microclimate regulation. Together, all these services have a substantial impact on the quality of life in our urban areas.

In this book, we will look at hands-on, small-scale ways to bring nature back to the city through your own yard, the area that most of us have the most control over. The content is aimed particularly at those of you living in the Pacific Northwest, which includes southern British Columbia, the states of Washington and Oregon, and a portion of Northern California. Each chapter offers fun, practical, and productive advice on how to build and maintain your green space based on eight key principles adopted from ecoPRO (see Resources):

1. Protect, conserve, and create healthy soil.
2. Maintain healthy plants and create a sustainable landscape.
3. Use sustainable methods and materials.
4. Conserve water.
5. Protect and enhance wildlife habitat.
6. Protect water and air quality.
7. Conserve energy.
8. Protect and enhance human health and well-being.

Every act is meaningful and has wide-ranging effects. For example, if you plant deciduous trees on the west-facing side of your house, they will create shade during hot summer months and thereby reduce the need for air-conditioning—and the associated costs and energy consumption. Protecting your existing native trees and shrubs means pre-serving indigenous biodiversity, and, besides that, they provide a buffer for noise pollution, improve air quality by processing cities' high outputs of harmful gases, diminish flooding by acting as natural barriers and bulwarks, and improve water quality by taking up and degrading pollutants. Growing your own food lessens the use of fossil fuels required for transporting produce from rural areas, particularly if you're composting and col-lecting rainwater for irrigation on site. And a vote for the care of parks and other natural areas in our cities is a vote for wildlife and

This quaint house nestled within the foliage stays cooler and is more aesthetically pleasing than a house without a garden.

LEFT: *A European honeybee visiting red clover* **RIGHT:** *An American goldfinch strikes a bright note in a crab apple tree.*

community entertainment, inspiration, and connection.

All of these acts can enhance the quality of life for urban dwellers and promote regional and community-based conservation and restoration. Whether you till your own little piece of land, tend a planter bed in a community garden, or support your local parks and rec department, you can help reduce the potential negative effects of climate change and create a healthy, vibrant, and resilient urban ecosystem.

CHAPTER CHECKLIST

☐ A healthy ecosystem is resilient, adaptive, and diverse.
☐ Nature provides ecosystem services that all life requires. These fall under the categories of supporting, provisioning, regulating, and cultural services.
☐ You can help preserve ecosystem services in eight key ways.

2

ASSESSING YOUR YARD

Your outdoor space may have a big lawn, a sprinkling of ornamental shrubs and perennials, and a large maple tree in one corner. Or perhaps you have a large patio with a barbecue pit and a few planter boxes and vases, a strip of lawn, and some small shrubs around the foundation of the house. Whatever your yard may look like, the fact that you've read this far probably means you are considering making a change.

Before you start your new garden or a garden renovation project, you need to formulate clear goals by asking yourself what you want to achieve. A gardener's goals for his or her garden are fourfold:

1. It should be both functional and visually pleasing.
2. It should be maintainable and cost effective.
3. It should be environmentally sound.
4. It should enhance biodiversity and create healthy habitats for wildlife.

Fortunately, when you are building a garden, you can look to a well-established role model—nature itself—to help you meet all of these goals and become an environmental steward. Designing by imitating natural systems will help you avoid degrading the surrounding environment while maximizing the support of ecological services. The integration of existing native vegetation, most likely already home to wildlife, with the vegetation you want to introduce

OPPOSITE: *Even a parking strip can be put to use as part of a garden.*

Take the time to create a detailed site map before you start making changes to your garden.

will enhance native wildlife habitat and biodiversity. Plus, thoughtfully chosen planting can help damaged areas return to their original vibrancy. You can speed up the healing process by using sustainable building materials, providing a permanent water source, allowing leaves and other organic matter to decompose on the surface of garden beds, and leaving rock piles, tree snags, brush, and woody debris on site.

I like to think of sustainable gardening as a combination of a rule and a philosophy. First, follow the Campsite Rule: leave the earth better than you found it. Add to that the practice of the Less Is More philosophy: make changes thoughtfully, and mostly just let Mother Nature do her job. A sustainable garden endures over time with minimal expenditure of energy and maintenance, while providing healthy habitats for native wildlife.

KNOW YOUR SITE

Before making any changes to your garden space, you need to know your site. The discovery process during your site assessment will help you understand your site's limitations and opportunities and thereby help you decide how to improve and design it. The better you know your site, the easier it will be for you to form a partnership with the environment and succeed in your gardening goals.

Start by evaluating the following key factors:

1. The physical and environmental features of the site
2. Plant health, function, and aesthetics
3. Potential maintenance efficiency and resource use

But don't get out your shovel and special gardening clogs just yet. Instead, grab your laptop or other such gadget, or a spiral-bound notebook and a pen, to record your observations. Creating a detailed garden journal containing a site inventory followed by a site analysis may feel like a big commitment at the beginning, but it will be worth it in the long run. Take your time with this; a thorough initial assessment will save you time and energy later.

Create a Site Map
The key first step is to determine the location, size, condition, and makeup of your site's existing features. I suggest you begin by constructing a map of your site that includes the property boundaries, house or other structures, electrical outlets and water sources, driveway, parking area, walkways, patio, lawn, planting beds, fences, current vegetation, and water features.

You should already have a property survey or site map of your parcel as part of the deed to your property. You may also find an aerial photo of your yard on Google Earth, or locate a topographical survey of your area from the United States Geological Survey. Whatever information is lacking can be filled in with the use of a tape measure, a carpenter's or laser site level, and a compass.

Start by plotting the overall width and length of the site and other rectangular shapes on your computer or on graph paper. Decide on a scale, such as 1 inch equals 10 feet for a small lot and 1 inch equals 20 or 40 feet for larger lots, to allow you to fit in the whole property and have enough space to detail the major site features. Use the house and other straight-lined shapes as reference points for other features on the site. For other landscape features, pick two fixed features such as a corner of your house and a corner of your patio, and from these two points measure the distance to the feature.

Once you have noted the size and location of key landscape features on your map, you will need to evaluate the site's topography. Knowing the steepness and direction of slopes as well as the drainage patterns will be useful later when you evaluate the microclimates on your site. If you are able to obtain a topographical map, it will show contour lines, with each line representing a specific elevation across the land. The difference in elevation between the contour lines is called the *rise*, while the distance between the lines is the *run*. The rise divided by the run indicates *slope*.

You can also estimate slope yourself using a 10-foot 2x4, a level, a weighted string, and a tape measure:

1. Lay the 2x4 on the slope, with one end at the top of the slope and the other end pointing straight down the slope.

2. Raise the lower end until it is perfectly level with the upper one; determine this by setting the level on the board.

3. Hang a weighted string from the end of the board and, using that string to make sure you are measuring straight down, measure the distance from the board to the ground with your tape measure.

4. To calculate slope by percentage, divide the rise by the run and multiply by 100. If the rise is 2 feet and the board is 10 feet long, then the slope is 20 percent ($2 \div 10 = 0.20$; $0.20 \times 100 = 20$).

5. Move the board 10 feet in one direction or the other, and repeat this process.

6. To get the average slope, sum up the rises and runs and divide the total rise by the total run. Multiply that by 100. However, if there are large differences in slopes or the slopes run in different directions, taking the average is not useful.

Next, use your compass to determine the direction the slope or slopes face. If possible, find out how far your site is above sea level with an online resource such as Free Map Tools.

Now locate the utilities on your property, both above- and belowground. *Before you start digging and planting your landscape, you must know the location of all possible obstruc-*

Once your board is level, measure from the bottom of the board to the ground.

LEFT: *A large area of impermeable paving creates a lot of unnecessary water runoff.* **RIGHT:** *Consider whether you can create a wider yet permeable walkway.*

tions or hazards. This includes electric, gas, water, and sewer lines, as well as the septic system (if applicable). Call 811, the number at which you can request someone to come and locate the underground utilities, pipes, and cables at your site, or contact your local utility companies and service providers to find out the location of underground pipes, electrical wires, and telephone and cable lines. Assess whether there are water or sewer easements crossing your property, and find out about the property restrictions associated with these easements. Determine where your underground drains go from your downspouts, and where they connect to your community's stormwater system, by asking your home builder, the previous homeowner, or the local utility company. Sketch in overhead wires to your site map too, so you can avoid planting trees that could ultimately interfere with them. Check whether there are any holes in the ground or obstructions sticking out of the ground that need to be filled or removed. Make a note of all of these observations in your notebook or folder.

Evaluate Site Conditions

Once you have a draft of your site map, it is time to evaluate the condition of the key landscape features—driveway, parking areas, paths, fences, and walls. Determine whether there are hazards on your property: Are walkways, patio, and driveway appropriately sized and located, functional and attractive, and suitable as access points? Are they uneven or posing a safety hazard? If you see something that needs fixing, make a note of action items in a separate folder.

If the driveway is the largest and most obvious feature of the yard, consider how much turnaround and parking space it has. If it's larger than it needs to be, you can reduce its impact on the site and the environment by reducing its size or replacing the hardscape in the center of it with vegetation (see Chapter 6, Sustainable Materials and Energy Choices). You may also

In this well-designed garden, trees and shrubs provide a living screen that offers shade and privacy.

want to enhance water infiltration by replacing the driveway's impermeable material with permeable material (see Chapter 7, Water).

Since you are going to need to move around as you improve and maintain your garden, check that the walkways are wide enough to accommodate a wheelbarrow or other garden equipment without hitting plants or other obstacles. Is there easy access to the planting beds or vegetable garden? If not, you may consider improving access by changing the garden paths or moving the location of the planting beds. Also, check whether the entryway to the front door is hidden from view or too narrow to allow two people to walk side by side (less than 4 feet). It's a good idea to have a clear and wide entryway, if possible.

If fencing and vegetation do not provide adequate privacy, or undesirable views are not adequately screened, you may want to include improved screening in your gardening project. On the other hand, does the site have any views that you particularly wish to preserve? Make a note of all these observations in your folder. Efforts to properly frame your borrowed scenery will naturally enhance the beauty of your garden.

If there is evidence of deer or other critters visiting for lunch and negatively impacting your plants, then this may indicate that you need to build a fence to protect your plants or augment the fence you already have.

Inventory Existing Plants

In the spring, summer, or fall, when deciduous plants still have their leaves, make a thorough inventory of the existing trees, shrubs, vines, groundcovers, and lawn. Before you make changes or improvements, you will need to decide which of these will be retained, transplanted, or removed. Are the plants healthy and aesthetically pleasing, with nice form and color? Do they have ideal soil, drainage, and sun exposure conditions? Once a given plant grows to maturity, will it fit its site location? If you have trees and woody shrubs that are healthy and aesthetically pleasing, planted in the right location, providing food and/or shelter for wildlife, and in accord with your gardening goals, it is important that you protect and preserve them.

Lawns usually take up a significant portion of the American yard and require considerable amounts of water and fertilizer, yet they provide little in the way of wildlife habitat. You should definitely consider downsizing your lawn or installing a more sustainable lawn requiring less water, fertilizer, and maintenance. (For information on how to make a more sustainable lawn, see Chapter 5, Ornamentals and Edibles.)

To create your inventory, start by determining the common name, size, and location of all trees at the site, including those beyond but near the property line. (If you need help identifying plants and properly evaluating their condition, contact your county extension office or master gardener clinic.) Estimate the height of your trees, and measure the spread of the canopy or mass of branches and leaves. Indicate whether the canopy is dense, moderately dense, or open. These observations will give you an idea of the area that will be blocked from sunlight. Areas under tree canopies are also usually quite dry, because the leaves block much of the rain from reaching the ground and the roots take up much of the available water and nutrients.

Record the same observations for woody shrubs and perennials. Place tags on your

When you do your plant inventory, consider keeping native plants such as the vine maple (left) but removing plants such as the nonnative butterfly bush (right).

woody plants, either with a number or the actual name of the plant. Permanent tags are available at many garden stores. While recording annuals, including vegetables, is not necessary, you may wish to make a note of groupings of herbaceous perennials (plants with nonwoody stems).

As you make this inventory, assess the health and condition of the plants: good, fair, poor, or dead? Is the plant diseased? (For more information on evaluating plant condition, see Chapter 9, Sustainable Care.) Additionally, ask whether the plant is attractive and useful or adequately serving its intended function, such as providing shade, defining a space, screening your neighbor's house, or enhancing wildlife habitat. If not, you may want to consider marking it for removal.

If possible, preserve plants that are already providing important habitat for wildlife:

Even a small wetland can provide a home for frogs and salamanders.

nectar- and pollen-rich wildflowers, flowering trees and shrubs, and nesting and egg-laying sites such as bare ground, stumps, nonhazardous snags, and old logs. Native plants are most likely to have accessible nectar and pollen for local pollinators, although many nonnative plants, such as the older varieties of perennials and annuals and many garden herbs, are good nectar and pollen sources as well. In fact, many native pollinators in the urban environment have become dependent on introduced plants because their native hosts are no longer available. However, if the plant has outgrown its allotted space, is too large relative to other plants nearby, or is overly aggressive, then consider marking it for removal.

Below is a summary of the information your plant inventory should contain for each plant you are recording. It's time to get started!

- Plant number and common name
- Scientific name of plant and cultivar
- Brief descriptive location (for example, "north side near patio")
- Size (particularly for trees and large shrubs)
- Condition of plant (good, fair, poor, dead)
- Decision about what to do with the plant (keep in place, transplant, remove, or thin) and why

Consider Environmental Factors

To make the most of your space and properly maintain your landscape, you need to consider the overall climate at your location, your garden's specific microclimates and topography, seasonal variation in sun and shade, soil type and condition, wind patterns, and how the water moves through the site.

Climate

The climate of the Pacific Northwest varies widely between western and eastern areas because of the significant influence of the Pacific Ocean in the west, which moderates the air temperature and is a major source of moisture, and the Olympic and Cascade mountain ranges, which deflect low-level air, alter precipitation patterns, and generally prevent the entry of cold air from the continental interior. Occasionally, cold air from the east can enter western Washington and Oregon from the Fraser River Valley or from the Columbia River Gorge.

Temperatures in the Northwest are largely determined by proximity to saltwater and by elevation. Seasonal variation in temperature is much greater east of the Cascade Range, about 60°F, while it is only about 30°F west of the Cascades. Most coastal areas between the Pacific Ocean and the Cascade mountains have a marine climate, in contrast to the semiarid to arid climate found east of the Cascades. By comparison with western areas, the eastern areas are characterized by much drier and colder winters, with yearly precipitation around 16 inches, average minimum temperatures from 0°F to 15°F, and substantially warmer summers; the relatively short growing season lasts about 100 to 180 days.

For the western portion of the Northwest, prevailing winds generally blow from the south or southwest during the wet season in late fall and winter, and from the northwest in summer. Yearly rainfall is about 35–45 inches in Puget Sound and the Willamette Valley, but only around 16 inches per year in the Olympic rain shadow. The western areas are characterized by long periods of drizzle and approximately 230 cloudy days per year but few thunderstorms or downpours. The precipitation regime is Mediterranean, with mild and very wet winters and cool and very dry summers, a wet season November through February, a dry season from July through September, and a transition period in spring and fall. As a consequence, plants for this region need to be adapted to a large amount of cold rain in winter and very little rain in summer. On average, the first frost occurs around mid-November and the last around mid-April. Consequently, the western portion of the Pacific Northwest has a mean of 200 days (range 150–250) of frost-free growing season, making it the best region in North America to grow a wide variety of perennials.

A plant's ability to grow in a region largely depends on its hardiness or ability to withstand a minimum low temperature. For this reason, the USDA has developed hardiness zones as a guide to gardeners based on the minimum 10-year-average winter temperatures. Plants are included in a hardiness zone if they are capable of withstanding

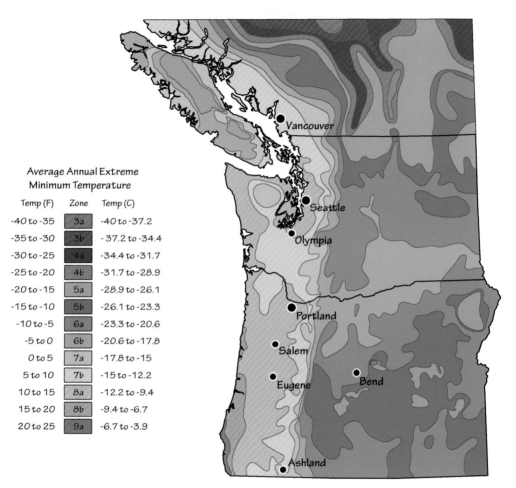

Average Annual Extreme Minimum Temperature

Temp (F)	Zone	Temp (C)
-40 to -35	3a	-40 to -37.2
-35 to -30	3b	-37.2 to -34.4
-30 to -25	4a	-34.4 to -31.7
-25 to -20	4b	-31.7 to -28.9
-20 to -15	5a	-28.9 to -26.1
-15 to -10	5b	-26.1 to -23.3
-10 to -5	6a	-23.3 to -20.6
-5 to 0	6b	-20.6 to -17.8
0 to 5	7a	-17.8 to -15
5 to 10	7b	-15 to -12.2
10 to 15	8a	-12.2 to -9.4
15 to 20	8b	-9.4 to -6.7
20 to 25	9a	-6.7 to -3.9

USDA hardiness zones for the Pacific Northwest

its minimum low temperature. The Pacific Northwest west of the Cascades has USDA hardiness zones of 7 to 9, with average winter minimums from roughly 0°F to 25°F, while east of the Cascades, USDA hardiness zones for the Pacific Northwest range from 4 to 7 with extreme minimums from -30°F to 10°F.

Although these hardiness guidelines are helpful, and you should take note of your hardiness zone, the actual minimum low temperature in your area may differ from year to year. Furthermore, these guidelines do not take into consideration elevation, precipitation, humidity, or latitude, which affect day length and have a significant impact on regional climates. Whether a plant can withstand a low temperature is also very much dependent on whether the plant has undergone winter acclimation or is dormant; actively growing plants are much more susceptible to cold temperatures. Also, windy conditions at low temperatures can make a plant more susceptible. Regardless of these limitations, you shouldn't expose a plant to a hardiness zone lower than it is rated—you would not want to place a plant zoned 8 to 9 in hardiness zone 7, where the low temperatures would quite likely damage or kill it.

Another climate-related resource is the American Horticultural Society Plant Heat Zone Map (see Resources), which will help you find your area's heat tolerance index. The map is based on the average yearly number of days on which temperatures exceed 86°F. However, this index has its limitations, and it does not consider the impact of the lack of water, air circulation, light, or day length, each of which can modify a plant's heat tolerance.

Accurately mapping the hardiness zones of the Pacific Northwest is difficult because of the wide variation in topography. The editors of *Sunset* magazine's *New Western Garden Book* have developed climate zones helpful to gardeners in the American West based on a broad range of factors: cold, summer heat, humidity, proximity to the Pacific Ocean, wind, snow cover, and length of growing season (see Resources).

The most relevant areas for the bulk of the Pacific Northwest population are Sunset climate zones 4, 5, and 6. Zone 4 is the cool maritime areas along the north coast, with wet winters and cool summers but slightly warmer in summer and colder in winter than neighboring zone 5. The Northwest Coast and Puget Sound, with wet, breezy winters and mild summers, covers zone 5. Zone 6 includes the Willamette and lower Columbia River valleys, with summer days averaging 80°F, a long growing season, and cool, wet winters.

Other sections of the Pacific Northwest include zone 1A, the coldest zone west of the Rockies, and zone 7, which includes Oregon's Rogue River Valley and the California Gray Pine Belt. For the specific locations of these zones, look up your Sunset climate zone map. I have indicated these zones for each plant in the plant lists in Chapters 4 and 5.

Microclimate

Because climate has a major influence on air and soil temperatures and precipitation during the growing season, take note in your garden journal of the following characteristics of your area:

1. Amount and seasonal variation of rainfall
2. Minimum low temperature in winter at sunrise
3. Maximum high temperature in summer in the shade about 4 feet off the ground
4. Date of the last frost in spring and first frost in fall
5. Sun and shade patterns during the day and through the seasons for each garden area

6. Speed and direction of prevailing winds during the different seasons

There can be microclimates even within the microclimate of your yard. Go back, for example, to your notes about the topography and elevation of your site: A valley between two large hills traps heavier cold air that slides down the slopes and forms a cold sink, leaving low-lying areas in your garden more prone to frost. Then again, if these low-lying areas are shaded they are less prone to frost, since shaded areas stay a few degrees warmer at night than unshaded ones.

Exposure

How your garden terrain orients to the sun has a major impact on specific temperatures in each garden area. The amount of solar energy a particular garden area receives depends on the number of hours of sunlight it gets and the angle at which the rays hit it. Since some plants need sun throughout the day, some do best in partial shade, and others tolerate full shade well, you need to consider the sun's path from morning till evening in the different seasons, so you can select the right plants based on sun and shade patterns. In the summer in northern latitudes the sun rises in the northeast, sits high in the southern sky at noon, and sets in the northwest. In winter the sun rises in the southeast, sits low in the southern sky at noon, and sets in the southwest. Thus, evergreen trees on the south side of your yard will shade a large portion of your garden, particularly in winter, when the sun is low in the sky.

Use a map or compass to determine the orientation or direction of your garden with regard to the sun. For example, my garden is on a southwest-facing slope that absorbs more solar energy, particularly in spring and fall, than gardens in the neighborhood with a different orientation. Garden areas with a northern or eastern orientation will absorb less sun energy and stay cooler; northern exposures will be moister in summer but more prone to frost in winter. Areas with eastern orientation are ideal for plants that prefer cool temperatures while still receiving a substantial amount of light. Areas with western exposure will be hotter and drier than other orientations.

Slope

As cold air moves down a slope it mixes with the warmer air; consequently, slopes are generally warmer than hilltops or valleys where cold air settles. Thus, full sun on a south- or southwest-facing slope should be ideal for warm-season vegetables and fruits. However, slope affects wind; my garden sits on a slope above a body of saltwater called the Port Washington Narrows and so receives considerably more wind than areas situated away from this body of water. The crest of the slope receives the most wind.

Determine whether your site is prone to windy conditions. Cold wind can dry out plants, particularly evergreens, and also contribute to broken branches and tree trunks. You can reduce its damaging impact by planting a windbreak. For more information on windbreaks, see Resources.

Drainage

The contour of your land can affect how well the soil drains and the kind of soil you have. A garden, like mine, that sits on a southwest slope and a hilltop generally drains well and warms earlier in the day and is warmer in each season than a flat garden, particularly on sunny days. However, by late summer this hillside becomes very dry, and the higher the elevation the drier the soil. In contrast, soils in low-lying areas are generally wetter than soils higher up.

During a rainstorm, assess your drainage patterns or direction of stormwater flow on and adjacent to the site. Where does the water flow and pool? Water pooling in low-lying areas may signal poor drainage that may require improvements in soil infiltration (see Chapter 3, The Living Soil). Dig a hole about a foot deep in the poorly draining area. If the soil looks gray and smells like rotting vegetation or rotten eggs, then this is indicative of poor drainage. Most plants thrive in soil where there is adequate air and water, but wet sites with poor drainage are deficient in oxygen. Indicate where water pools on your map. For more information on what to do about poorly draining sites, see Chapter 3.

Soil Depth and Compaction

Soil depth, an important factor in plant growth, varies with location and elevation. Low-lying areas in the Pacific Northwest generally have deep, well-developed soils (assuming that they have not been altered by development), while soils at higher elevations and on hilltops are generally shallower

You don't have to live with poor drainage!

Tomatoes growing near a west facing wall soak up the afternoon heat and receive heat released from the wall at night.

and more likely to be nutrient-deficient. To estimate soil depth, pick an area where the soil is undisturbed and, when the soil is moist, begin digging with a spade until you hit a barrier other than small rocks. Measure and record the depth of the hole, and repeat the process in several other patches of undisturbed soil in your yard. The average of these measures will be an estimate of your soil depth.

Compaction, a relatively common occurrence in urban soils, can restrict the soil depth that a plant can use. Evidence of erosion, such as narrow and shallow channels on the soil surface or soil deposits at the bottom of slopes, suggests compacted soil and/or excessive stormwater runoff. To get some idea of the degree of compaction in different areas of the garden, see Chapter 3. Mark areas that may have significant compaction on your site map.

Other Features

Unique features at your site, such as large rocks, outcrops, or walls, can affect microclimate. A south- or southwest-facing wall will release heat at night, even if you are in an area with cool summers, and create a good place for warm-season vegetables. However, areas north of the wall will be shady, and if solid, the wall can significantly alter wind patterns.

Research Your Site's History

If possible, find out about the history of the site by asking neighbors who have lived in your area for a long time or the previous owners of your home. Has human activity affected the site's topography? For example, was grading done that resulted in removal of native soil, or were artificial mixes or fill material added to the site? If so, what was the nature of this material? Is there any evidence that the area was exposed to harmful chemicals or heavy metals or received significant applications of fertilizers or pesticides?

If there are a lot of weeds present, this may indicate lot grading in the past, removal of existing vegetation, or addition of fill material, since disturbing healthy soils can damage soil structure and raise weed seeds to the surface, where they will germinate. Furthermore, plants that are growing poorly, or the presence of invasive species, may suggest that the soil has been disturbed and needs improvement. On the other hand, if there are minimal weeds present and your plants appear healthy, then it is likely you have good-quality soil. As you will see in Chapter 3, good soil is essential for healthy plants. If healthy native plants are growing on the site, you may have native soil.

Gauge Maintenance Efficiency and Resource Use

To improve maintenance efficiency and reduce resource use, the first step is to carefully evaluate what you are doing now to maintain your yard. Ask yourself the following questions:

- How much time does it take to mow my lawn, and how often do I mow it?
- How much water is required to saturate my lawn, and how often do I water it, particularly in summer?

- What is the frequency and duration of my other watering tasks, such as watering flower and shrub beds, or my vegetable garden? (To estimate water usage for irrigation, calculate the difference between winter and summer water usage.)
- How often and to what extent do I add fertilizer to these different yard areas?
- How much time do I spend weeding, mulching, cleaning, deadheading, dividing, and pruning plants and raking leaves?
- How much time do I spend removing or transplanting plants?
- About how many hours per week does it take to maintain my garden and hardscapes in the different seasons?

Once you have answered these questions, you will have a fairly good idea of your current maintenance requirements and use of resources.

BRAINSTORM NEXT STEPS

Once you have thoroughly assessed the condition of your site, you can figure out what management practices will best enable you to create a yard that is easier on the earth and good for wildlife. Begin with soil, by working to create healthy soil (Chapter 3, The Living Soil), then you can plant and maintain native and site-appropriate nonnative trees and plants (Chapter 4, Trees, and Chapter 5, Ornamentals and Edibles) that are compatible with the site's microclimates. This will increase plant diversity and provide a sustainable and wildlife-friendly sanctuary right out your back door (Chapter 8, Urban Wildlife Sanctuary).

You can protect and restore natural processes by minimizing the use of potable water. Do this by using low-water-use plants, harvesting rainwater, and using efficient irrigation and *graywater*, relatively clean water without fecal contamination from bathtubs, sinks, showers, and washing machines. You can also improve water quality by minimizing the amount of stormwater that leaves the site, reducing impermeable surfaces, and enhancing water infiltration (Chapter 7, Water).

You can reduce your yard's carbon footprint and convert a resource-hungry landscape into one that's better for the environment by using sustainable methods and materials and by conserving energy and improving air quality (Chapter 6, Sustainable Materials and Energy Choices). You can also remove high-maintenance plants and reduce or remove the lawn to minimize water and fertilizer use and labor (Chapter 5, Ornamentals and Edibles).

To lend structure to your gardening plan, write down your specific long-range goals for the landscape and make a list of site modifications you would like to see accomplished. Be specific about which tasks to tackle first. Include your best estimate of the cost for each task and the numbers of hours or days you expect it will take you to complete it.

CHAPTER CHECKLIST

- ☐ Create a site map of your yard, including and labeling property boundaries, the house and other landscape features, and topography.
- ☐ Evaluate the condition of features like driveway, patio, fences, walls, walkways.
- ☐ Inventory your existing plants in a spreadsheet with plant names, locations, sizes, conditions, and future plans.
- ☐ Evaluate your regional climate, and your yard's microclimate, slope, and history.
- ☐ Analyze your maintenance efficiency and use of resources.
- ☐ Brainstorm specific projects that you want to tackle.

PART 2

MAKING CHANGES

3

THE LIVING SOIL

In the soil beneath your feet, diverse groups of organisms work day and night to support all the life-forms that live above it. The soil is the home of a living, breathing, teeming collective whose health is absolutely essential to, well, everyone. Yet most of us humans largely ignore it, except when we need to wash it off our hands or out of our clothes.

Urban soils often lack this necessary biodiversity of tenants, due to the way people have affected their chemical properties, structural profile, and water drainage. Building structures, cleaning or painting houses, maintaining cars, and deicing walkways introduce heavy metals and other damaging substances into the soil. Chemical fertilizers, herbicides, insecticides, and fungicides can further harm the habitats of soil organisms, and past farming or industry use may have left toxic residues.

Urban soils can have a different pH (acidity or alkalinity level) than native soils. During development, the excavation of a foundation or leveling of the land usually brings up subsurface soils, which are then dumped on top of the original soils. Bland filler materials, such as gravel and sand, are often added to the mix. This creates *horizons*—layers of vastly different soil types, density, or textures—which can form soil interfaces that interfere with root growth and inhibit movement of water and nutrients. For instance, roots in a looser soil might not be able to grow into adjacent denser soil, such as heavy clay, and as a consequence the tree cannot root as deeply as it should and can become unhealthy and a safety hazard. Or water might get trapped in one soil layer and be unable to penetrate to deeper layers.

OPPOSITE: *Garden snails in a sustainable garden are part of the natural balance.*

LEFT: *Topsoil is removed for new construction and the remaining soil is compacted by heavy equipment.*
RIGHT: *Healthy, loamy soil*

Healthy, fertile, plant-plenty soils contain an astounding abundance of organisms. When you pick up a handful of such soil, you are holding a complex community of microscopic prey, predators, decomposers, and nutrient transformers, a world that's mostly invisible yet as real and dramatic as your dog chasing the neighbor's cat or scaring the deer away from your yard. The soil organisms' complicated enterprises make up the busy universe of the soil.

LITTLE CRITTERS

Soil contains about one-quarter or more of all life-forms on the planet, yet these life-forms are the least known and most neglected. Soil organisms—bacteria, fungi, earthworms, and more—have an important job to do: They are nature's primary decomposers. They convert the organic material of dead plants, carbohydrates, and other compounds into nutrients,

energy, carbon dioxide, and water to fuel new plant life. Together, plants and soil organisms create a cycle in which four critical functions occur:

- Organic matter is decomposed.
- Nutrients are captured and made useful.
- Soil structure is maintained in the form of aggregates of mineral particles and the channels between them.
- The populations of soil organisms, including pests and the organisms that cause disease, are regulated.

Following is a closer look at who these soil organisms are, and what they do.

Microorganisms: Bacteria and Fungi
Microorganisms are the smallest group, on average less than 0.02 millimeter. Bacteria and fungi are the best-known of this bunch.

Bacteria

Bacteria—tiny, single-celled organisms—are among the most abundant and diverse groups of soil organisms. Some 10,000 species are known, and likely many more are yet to be discovered; a single teaspoon of fertile soil contains many millions of bacteria.

Bacteria maintain soil structure, cycle nutrients, help control plant pests and diseases, remove soil pollutants, and reduce the need for watering plants. To be active and move within the soil matrix, they require a thin layer of water held around soil particles by adhesion. Some bacteria produce a slime that binds small particles together to form larger, more stable soil aggregates that improve water infiltration and the soil's water-holding capacity. This, of course, benefits the plants, which the bacteria eat and then digest, processing proteins, sugars, organic carbon, and nitrogen compounds. Later, when other organisms in the soil feed on the bacteria, they ingest these nutrients in their new viable form. Some bacterial decomposers can even break down—and thus detoxify—pollutants and pesticides.

A few plant species, such as legumes (plants in the pea family) and some tree species, host *Rhizobium* on nodes on their roots. These specialized nitrogen-fixing bacteria convert nitrogen gas from the air to ammonium, a form that can be used by most trees, shrubs, and perennials. Other specialized nitrifying bacteria convert ammonium to nitrate, the form of nitrogen that most annuals, vegetables, and grasses need. Other mutualistic symbiotic bacteria stimulate plant growth by producing plant hormones, while some can help control plant disease.

In addition to cycling nitrogen, bacteria also recycle other elements, such as carbon and sulfur. Not all soil bacteria are beneficial, however: some are bacterial pathogens, like those that cause gall, or abnormal growths, in plants. In healthy ecosystems that contain diverse bacterial communities, beneficial organisms can help modulate the populations of disease-causing ones.

Fungi

Fungi are generally made up of a group of cells that grow as fine threads, or *hyphae*, and join in a network called a *mycelium*. Hyphae bind soil particles together to create structure that supports the flow of water. Because, unlike bacteria, they do not need a water film to move through soil, fungi provide nutrients and water to plants when conditions are too dry for bacteria to be active. Fungi are aerobic organisms, however. Compacted or waterlogged soil often lacks oxygen; in these soils fungal activity slows or stops.

Fungi are the primary decomposers in the soil's food web of complex organic compounds. They process organic material and return carbon and nitrogen compounds to the ecosystem in forms usable to plants, insects, and other organisms. Unlike bacteria, fungi can decompose cellulose and lignin in wood, as well as the complex organic

Mushrooms help break down complex organic compounds in soil and capture nutrients from the soil, while the mycelium from some mushrooms provides nutrients and water to plants. On the negative side, if the mushrooms are poisonous, they could potentially pose a hazard to young children or pets.

compounds of some soil pollutants, rendering them nontoxic.

Most terrestrial plant species have *mycorrhizae*, the beneficial symbiotic partnership between fungi and living plant roots. In effect, the mycorrhiza is the bridge between the plant and the soil; the fungi receive sugars and other carbon-containing compounds produced by the plant, and in return they make water and other soil nutrients available to the plant. They also extend the effective surface area and reach of plant roots, which greatly helps plants resist drought and take up nutrients. Mycorrhizae also enhance plant resistance to root pathogens and soilborne pests and diseases, and boost tolerance of heavy-metal contamination.

Though their effect on the larger ecosystem is generally beneficial, some fungi are parasites or cause disease. The fungus *Botrytis cinerea* causes gray mold in many herbaceous annual and perennial plants, perhaps most notably on wine grapes when conditions are too humid. The fungi *Verticillium albo-atrum* and *Verticillium dahliae* attack a large variety of herbaceous and woody plant species, causing the dreaded verticillium wilt. Other parasitic fungi, however, are beneficial, as they feed on disease-causing nematodes or harmful insects.

Microfauna

Microfauna are the smallest of the soil fauna and, at between 0.02 and 0.1 millimeter in size, are largely invisible to the naked eye. The best-known members of this group are the protozoa and nematodes. They feed on bacteria and fungi, modulate bacteria populations, and make nitrogen, phosphorous, and other essential compounds more available to plants. Protozoa and nematodes tend to share the same niche in the soil ecosystem—the water film surrounding soil particles and within soil pores.

Protozoa

Protozoa are single-celled organisms that move through the water-filled pores. Most of them eat bacteria, but some feed on fungi or other soil organisms. Some are *saprophytic*, meaning they feed on particulate organic matter. In their waste products, protozoa excrete a significant proportion of the nitrogen and other nutrients that plants need.

Nematodes

Nematodes are small, nonsegmented roundworms that live in water films in large pore spaces or adjacent to plant roots. There may be fifty different species in a single handful of soil. As they move through the soil, they transport bacteria or fungi on their surfaces or in their digestive systems. Because of their relatively large size, they are more common in coarse-textured soils with large pore spaces. Different species have specialized mouthparts that vary depending on their feeding habits. Some nematodes feed on plants and algae, others feed on bacteria and fungi, still others

eat other nematodes and small members of the soil food web. Nematodes also kill insect larvae by injecting them with the bacteria living inside their guts. In turn, nematodes are prey for higher-level predators, such as insects and small arthropods.

Mesofauna

Soil mesofauna are invertebrates between 0.1 and 2 millimeters in size. Unlike microfauna, they are visible to the naked eye. They live in the soil or in the litter layer on the surface of the soil. Typical members of this group are the mites and springtails. They play an important part in the carbon cycle.

Mites

Mites belong to a subgroup of arthropods called arachnids, which, like spiders, have hard bodies and eight legs. They inhabit air-filled soil pores and litter layers. Mites play an important role in the soil food web. Some feed on plants and algae, some feed on bacteria and fungi, and some are predators that feed on nematodes, other mites, springtails, and the larvae of insects.

Springtails

Springtails—primitive insects with no wings—belong to another subgroup of arthropods, the insects, which have three pairs of legs and one pair of antennae. Like mites, they live in air-filled soil pores and litter layers. Unlike mites, they require high humidity and feed primarily on fungi

and algae, although some are predators. Springtails serve as a food source for other organisms and are particularly abundant in rangeland and many agricultural soils.

Macrofauna

The members of the macrofauna group tend to be larger than 2 millimeters and include many types of arthropods and soft-bodied, legless soil creatures, such as gastropods (e.g., slugs and snails), and annelids such as earthworms. They function as decomposers and shredders, predators, herbivores, and ecosystem engineers. For example, millipedes, sowbugs, beetles, and termites decompose and shred particulate and dissolved dead organic matter. Spiders, ants, centipedes, and ground beetles are all predators that feed on insects and other small animals. Many insects are herbivores and feed on plants and roots. Other macrofauna, like earthworms, ants, and termites, are the major ecosystem engineers in soil and profoundly affect soil structure by tunneling and digging.

Earthworms

There are three major types of earthworms. These include small worms, which live on or near the surface litter layer; worms that live in the upper soil layer, eat organic matter,

TOP: *Earthworms are valuable residents of your garden's soil.* MIDDLE: *Although they damage plants by eating the leaves, slugs also provide food for all kinds of birds, mammals, insects, and soil organisms.* BOTTOM: *Ants contribute to the soil's porosity.*

and make temporary channels that become filled with their excreta; and deep-burrowing species that make permanent tunnel systems throughout the soil layers. The deeper species primarily feed on surface organic matter, pulling it down into their burrows and mixing it with the soil. Their comparatively large tunnels provide channels for root growth and significantly increase soil aeration, porosity, water infiltration, and water-holding capacity. They also consume a large amount of mineral particles. Their excreta, in the form of castings, provide shredded organic matter and nutrients that other soil-dwelling organisms consume.

Termites and Ants

Like earthworms, termites and ants cause gross physical changes to the soil and affect the diversity and abundance of other soil organisms. Termites are more abundant in subtropical or tropical parts of the world. They decompose wood and other dead plant material and play an important role in cycling nutrients. Their foraging and tunneling activity enhances soil porosity and water infiltration. Similarly, soil-nesting ants increase soil porosity and movement of water and nutrients through the soil. Ants are also responsible for dispersing the seeds of many plants.

LIVING SPACES FOR LITTLE CRITTERS: SOIL PORES AND TEXTURE

All of these little critters live amid the minerals and organic matter—other live plants and organisms, as well as dead ones—within the soil, usually in the top 4 to 6 inches, which has more pore spaces than lower soil horizons do.

Large pores conduct air, water, and nutrients throughout the soil and thereby determine a soil's permeability and aeration. Small pores are responsible for the soil's water-holding capacity. This incredibly dynamic pore network is in constant flux, shrinking and swelling due to changes in moisture and temperature that result in freezing and thawing. Growing roots help create the pores, as do the soil inhabitants.

The amount of pore space within particles of soil varies with *soil texture*, a term that refers to the relative proportion of three different sizes of mineral particles: larger, coarse-textured sand particles; intermediate silt particles; and smaller, fine-textured clay particles. In contrast, *soil structure* refers to how soil particles are aggregated, or combined.

Soil texture influences important properties of the soil, such as its water-holding capacity, organic matter content, aeration, drainage, and susceptibility to erosion. For example, soils high in sand content have big spaces between the large sand particles, and are therefore fast draining and vulnerable to drought and have poor nutrient retention. A cubic foot of sand stores only about 1.2 inches of water per foot of soil depth. Even though this is a small quantity, most of it is available to plants. Well-drained, sandy soil generally has good aeration, or pockets of air, which is conducive to healthy plant growth, but organic matter breaks down faster. In contrast, soils high in clay have small pores that enable them to store a lot of water, approximately 3.9 inches of water per foot of soil depth for a cubic foot of clay soil. But these soils are not as permeable to air, and only about 1.5 inches of water per foot of soil is available to plants. Clay-rich soils are prone to compaction and poor water movement and are more susceptible to erosion than sandy soils; however, clay soil has the best nutrient retention. Silt soils have fairly good water-holding capacity, slightly less than clay soils, but the amount of plant-available water is greater than in clay or sandy soil. The aeration and drainage in silty soil is reasonable, somewhat greater than in clay soil, but not as good as in sandy soil. However, silt soils erode readily. Silt soil has intermediate nutrient retention.

Determining Soil Texture in Your Garden

Knowing what kind of soil texture you have will help you provide better care for your plants. You can get a general idea of your soil's texture by observing its physical characteristics through a ribbon test, or performing a jar test. As soil texture can vary throughout the garden, take samples from several different garden areas, such as lawns and planting beds, and repeat the tests for each sample.

Ribbon Test

1. Pick up a handful of soil, and slowly add water to it until the soil is moldable like putty.

2. Rub the soil between your fingers. If the soil feels gritty, it contains predominantly sand. If it feels smooth, silt dominates, while clay soil feels sticky.

3. With the ball molded into a cigar shape in the palm of your hand, gently squeeze it out between your thumb and index finger, extruding a ribbon of uniform thickness. If it bends and then breaks at a length of at least 3.5 inches, you have silty clay soil; soils that feel in between gritty and smooth but can generate a ribbon of 3.5 inches contain predominantly clay. When wetted, soils that are predominantly clay hold together and can form into a ball. Soils containing mostly sand feel gritty and crumble, even when moist.

Jar Test

A more quantitative approach to determining soil texture is the jar test.

1. Fill a clean, clear quart jar about two-thirds full of water, and add a teaspoon of powdered dishwashing detergent.

2. Bring this mixture, along with a shovel and a plastic bucket, to your outdoor space.

3. Remove grass and roots from a spot about 6 inches in circumference, then

In this jar test for soil texture, three soil layers are visible: sand at the bottom, silt in the middle, and clay on top.

dig a hole about 8 inches deep with straight vertical sides. Take off a slice of soil about 1 inch thick from the side of the hole and place it in the bucket. Remove all rocks, roots, and other debris from this soil sample. Repeat this process by taking slices of soil from holes in other areas of the garden, removing all rocks and debris, and adding the soil to the bucket.

4. Stir up the soil in the bucket, and then transfer enough of this mixed soil to nearly fill the quart jar.

5. Tighten the jar lid and invert the jar back and forth, shaking vigorously until all the soil particles are suspended.

6. Leave the jar upright on a level surface for 48 hours to let the soil particles settle.

7. With the soil now settled, you should see three layers: a bottom sand layer, an intermediate silt layer, and a top layer of clay with perhaps some organic matter floating on top. Use a ruler to measure the thickness of each layer and the total depth of the soil comprising all three layers.

8. To determine the proportion of each layer as a percentage, divide the depth of each layer by the total depth of all three layers, and multiply each of the numbers by 100. If you have trouble

clearly discerning the top of the sand or silt layer you can vigorously remix the soil to suspend all the soil particles. Let the jar sit for 1 minute and measure the depth of the bottom sand layer. After 30 minutes measure the depth of the settled soil. From this depth subtract the depth of the sand layer to obtain the depth of the intermediate silt layer. The remaining unsettled particles that represent the clay layer can be calculated by subtracting the sand and silt layers from the total depth obtained in step 7.

A good garden loam contains about equal proportions of sand and silt and about 8 to 30 percent clay. As a result, it has a balance of large, intermediate, and small pores, and it generally has near-optimal water infiltration, water-holding capacity, nutrient retention, and drainage. This is what you want to have in your garden. If you don't have this ideal balance in your soil particles it is not practical to thoroughly alter your soil's texture. You can, however, ameliorate less than ideal soil conditions, such as too much clay, sand, or silt, by incorporating compost into your soil. Adding compost to clay or silt soil makes the soil more porous, improving aeration, drainage, and water infiltration; compost in sandy soil acts like a sponge to slow drainage and improve water retention. Compost also provides nutrients for all the soil critters. Providing nutrients, habitat pores, air, and water to all the critters in soil makes for healthy soil and healthy plants. For more on compost, see DIY Composting, later in this chapter.

Soil Drainage

Compacted soil is a relatively common problem in the built environment. The weight of construction equipment tamps down soil during development, and foot traffic continues the problem. This commonly causes poor drainage in urban areas; other factors, such as problematic soil interfaces created during construction and fill activities, can also play a role in poor drainage.

An easy way to determine whether your garden has poor drainage is to see if standing water tends to collect in low-lying areas after a rain. Or assess the degree of compaction by taking a steel rod, such as rebar or a soil probe, and seeing how many inches you can push it into the soil in different regions of your yard. If it goes in a few inches, the ground is hard and compacted. If it goes in nearly 8 inches there is little compaction; an intermediate level (4–6 inches) indicates moderate compaction.

A more active and comprehensive approach is to determine your soil's actual percolation rate. Perform this test when the soil is not excessively wet or dry; in the Northwest, springtime is best. To test your entire yard, dig several holes in different locations around your yard and perform the test in each place.

LEFT and RIGHT: *For the percolation test, placing a board across the top of the hole gives you a clear way to measure the depth of the water as it drains.*

Percolation Test

1. Dig a hole 12 inches deep and 12 inches in diameter, with straight vertical sides.
2. Saturate the soil by filling the hole with water several times within 1 day, without necessarily letting it fully drain between each time. Then let the water completely drain overnight.
3. Refill the hole to within an inch or two of the top.
4. Allow the hole to drain 2 to 4 inches, then measure the height of the water with a yardstick or ruler. Check the time.
5. Allow the water to drain approximately 2 to 6 more inches for 1 to 4 hours, and note the time it takes for this to happen. Measure the height of the water again.
6. Calculate the average drop in water per hour. For example, if the water drops 6 inches in 3 hours, divide 6 by 3: the water drains 2 inches per hour.

What do these numbers mean?

- If the soil drains less than ½ inch per hour, your drainage is too slow.
- If the soil drains between 1 and 3 inches per hour, the drainage is adequate.
- If the soil drains more than 6 inches per hour, the drainage is too fast and will tend to be susceptible to drought.

Improving Soil Drainage

One way to begin to improve soil drainage and decrease compaction is to mix compost into the soil. This will, in most instances, increase the soil's pore space. In the Pacific Northwest, the best time to break up compacted

Frequently turn compost with a spading fork to promote aeration and speed its decomposition.

soil is before the soil completely dries out, usually in May or early June. If you break up or till the soil when it is wet, you risk damaging its structure and increasing the rate at which organic matter in the soil decomposes, reducing its nutrient holding capacity.

1. Use a spading fork to break apart compacted soil to a depth of 12 to 18 inches. The depth will depend on the extent of compaction and/or inadequate drainage, and on what you are planning to plant. At this time you may not know what you expect to plant, but if you know you are planting trees or shrubs, it is best to loosen the soil down to 18 inches, while 12 inches should be adequate for most other plantings.

2. Do not break up the soil too finely, as doing so can destroy its delicate structure. The spading fork is least likely to cause damage.

3. Add approximately 3 inches of high-quality compost to the newly broken-up soil to reduce compaction and improve structure and pore space. Mix it in with the spading fork.

4. Top with a coarse organic mulch to minimize additional compaction.

Depending on the severity of the drainage problem, you may want to investigate alternate solutions:

- Installing underground drainage pipes: This involves digging trenches about 2 feet deep through the area and installing drainage pipe with gravel placed below and above them. The water from this drainage bed must then be directed to a storm drain, rain garden, or other water retention facility (see Chapter 7, Water).

- Building a raised bed for vegetables and flowers: This is a practical solution for small areas; see Chapter 5, Ornamentals and Edibles, for more information.

- Creating a bog garden by adding moisture-loving plants to this wet area: See the Bog Garden Planting Plan sidebar.

SOIL FOOD

The relative acidity or alkalinity of soil is referred to as *pH*. Simply put, this is a marker

BOG GARDEN PLANTING PLAN

If you have a permanently moist area in your garden, you can adapt it by planting a bog garden and thereby creating valuable wildlife habitat. Examples of plants suitable for a bog garden are listed here.

PLANT	FORM	SIZE	BLOOM TIME	COLOR
NATIVE PLANTS				
Bog laurel (*Kalmia occidentalis*)	Evergreen shrub	1–3 ft. tall and wide	Late spring	Pink to rose
Red-twig dogwood (*Cornus sericea*)	Deciduous shrub	10 ft. tall and wide	Late spring	White
Douglas spirea (*Spiraea douglasii*)	Deciduous shrub	3–6 ft. tall and wide	Summer	Pink
Monkey flower (*Mimulus guttatus, Mimulus cardinalis*)	Herbaceous perennial	1–3 ft. tall and wide	Spring and summer	Yellow or red
Pacific ninebark (*Physocarpus capitatus*)	Deciduous shrub	8–12 ft. tall and wide	Late spring	White
NONNATIVE PLANTS				
Cardinal flower (*Lobelia cardinalis*)	Herbaceous perennial	2–4 ft. tall x 1–2 ft. wide	Summer	Red
Fleece flower (*Persicaria amplexicaulis* 'Golden Arrow')	Herbaceous perennial	4 ft. tall x 3 ft. wide	Summer and fall	Red
Siberian iris (*Iris sibirica*)	Herbaceous perennial	3 ft. tall x 2 ft. wide	Late spring and summer	Blue
Forget-me-not (*Myosotis scorpioides*)	Herbaceous perennial	6–12 in. tall x 12–24 in. wide	Early summer	Light blue
Tatting fern 'Frizelliae' (*Athyrium filix-femina*)	Fern	22 in. tall and wide	n/a	n/a

Growing vegetables in a raised bed surrounded with copper pipe to create a slug barrier is a practical solution for sites with poor drainage.

of how well plants use the nutrients in the soil. It is measured on a scale of 1 to 14, with lower numbers indicating acidity and higher numbers indicating alkalinity or basicity; a pH of 7 is considered neutral.

Because pH is on a logarithmic scale, a pH of 5 is ten times more acidic than a pH of 6. Most plants grow best in the pH range of 6.3 to 6.8, although many can adapt to soils that are more acidic or more alkaline. Plants that like acid soil include azaleas, camellias, heaths and heathers, and rhododendrons; clematis, daphne, dianthus, and lilacs prefer alkaline soil. Note that bacterial activity increases in warmer weather and causes pH to decrease, so soil pH tends to be lower (more acidic) in summer and higher in winter.

Knowing the pH of your soil is useful because pH determines the availability of nutrients, and it can affect the relative abundance of beneficial and harmful soil organisms. You can find inexpensive soil test kits at your local garden store or nursery, and they contain detailed instructions on how to use them.

Testing Soil pH

To test the soil pH, it is important to take several representative samples from each garden area, such as a vegetable bed, a lawn, and/or a planting bed. Take soil from the surface but below any mulch layer you may have, to the depth of the root zone for each area: 6 inches down for the vegetable bed, 4 inches for established lawns, and 8 inches for the planting bed.

1. Take a sample of dry soil from each site with a clean hand trowel or a soil probe, then mix the subsamples together in a jar.
2. Take a tablespoon from this mixture and place it in another jar. Clearly label the jar.
3. Add 4 tablespoons of distilled water to the second jar and mix, then wait for a few minutes to allow the mixture to settle.
4. Transfer some of the mixture to the test kit's color comparator, and add the indicator powder as directed. Watch the color develop.
5. To estimate the pH value, match that color to the kit's chart.

If preliminary analysis identifies particularly large areas where the pH is outside the 6.3–6.8 range, which is optimal for most plants, consider having the soil professionally analyzed to make sure your measurement is correct. At the same time, learn the pH requirements of the existing plants—their state of health may be indicative of the pH, along with the test. When you know what plants you want to plant as well as their optimal pH requirements, you can take remedial action to adjust the soil's pH if necessary.

In many cases, it may be better to adjust the selection of the plants around the kind of soil you have, rather than go to all the effort of altering the pH with chemicals for the sake of the plants. However, there are several relatively simple ways to adjust pH:

- To raise pH, add small amounts of dolomite lime containing magnesium, which you can obtain at home improvement stores such as Lowe's or Home Depot. Follow the instructions on the bag regarding the quantity to apply (usually 5 pounds per 100 square feet).

- Before attempting to lower pH, check your soil for concrete or other foreign substances that may contribute to a high pH (soils containing soft limestone naturally tend to be more alkaline). If they're present, remove them, then add compost and retest the soil's pH after several months. If after that time the soil is still too alkaline, add small amounts of aluminum sulfate or elemental sulfur from your local garden store or nursery; follow the instructions on the bag. This is an effective but temporary solution. It's best to add the sulfur in summer when the soil is warm. The pH lowers immediately when aluminum sulfate dissolves in the soil, but it may take weeks or several months if you use sulfur.

Testing Organic Matter and Nutrient Levels

The color of your soil provides an index of its organic matter content. The more organic matter that is present, the darker the soil.

Soil test kits reveal the characteristics of your soil and what it might need. To get your

NITROGEN

Nitrogen is an essential component of key organic molecules such as nucleic acids and proteins, which are necessary for life, and chlorophyll, which is required for photosynthesis and plant growth. It is a crucial element for plant growth and development, biodiversity, and ecosystem functions.

The nitrogen cycle is the process by which living organisms and their physical environment convert nitrogen into its various forms. Although nitrogen gas is abundant, making up about 78 percent of the atmosphere, it is not usable by most plants in that form. Instead, plants—and nearly all organisms from prey and predators to decomposers—must rely on nitrogen gas that is "fixed" or bonded to hydrogen or oxygen to form primarily ammonium and nitrate. A small, select group of plants, bacteria, and algae do the fixing.

The burning of fossil fuels releases nitrogen-containing gases into the atmosphere, and the burning of forests, wood fuels, and grasslands liberates nitrogen from its long-term biological storage pools. Agricultural activities have replaced large swaths of natural vegetation with nitrogen-fixing crops like legumes, putting even more nitrogen into these areas. But by far the largest human contribution to the global nitrogen cycle is industrial fertilizers, whose production process requires a lot of energy and emits substantial quantities of greenhouse gases.

Because of human activity, the amount of nitrogen in terrestrial ecosystems has doubled in the past century. This means more nitrogen oxides, smog, acid rain, and acid soil; fewer soil nutrients such as calcium and potassium; and the leaching of nitrates into coastal waters. Plus, we've lost many of the plants adapted to use nitrogen efficiently.

There are a few ways that the local city-dwelling gardener can help reduce nitrogen use:

- Apply organic fertilizer only when absolutely needed, based on a soil or plant tissue test or on an examination of the plant. Add the minimum amount of nitrogen needed as determined by the soil testing.
- Add any necessary nitrogen in small doses over several applications.
- Add nitrogen-containing fertilizer in the spring to minimize leaching of nitrates from the soil, particularly in maritime climates with ample rain.
- In a vegetable garden, alternate between nitrogen-fixing crops (such as legumes) and all those that don't fix nitrogen (the majority of crops). This will minimize the need for nitrogen-containing fertilizers.

soil's organic matter content and nutrient levels tested, consult your county conservation district or county extension agent for certified soil-testing facilities in your area. Washington State's King County Conservation District provides up to five free soil tests per resident, which are analyzed by A & L Western Agricultural Laboratories in Portland, Oregon. If you live outside of King County or Washington State, you can send your samples directly to that laboratory (see Resources).

The basic soil test kit from A & L provides the following information: the soil's pH, its organic matter content, its cation exchange capacity (the soil's ability to hold a reserve supply of nutrients), and its amounts of the primary nutrients nitrogen, phosphorus, and potassium, secondary nutrients sulfur, calcium, and magnesium, and soil-extractable sodium. The results are accompanied by specific recommendations for your plant needs.

A soil test kit should include detailed instructions for how to perform it. Here are my own recommendations:

1. Perform the test between September 15 and October 15, when the soil is not overly water saturated.

2. Take samples from different areas in your yard, just as you would for a jar test or pH test. Avoid areas that have been recently treated with fertilizer, compost, or lime.

3. Take multiple samples (ten or more) randomly but evenly distributed across each garden area. If using a trowel, first make a V-shaped hole. If sampling in the fall, dig 12 inches; at other times of the year dig 4 inches for lawn, 6 inches for vegetable gardens, and 8 inches near trees or shrubs.

4. Take the soil in thin slices (about ½ inch) down to the selected depth.

5. Thoroughly mix the subsamples collected in a given garden area, and place 2 or 3 cups of the mixed soil—or the amount specified by the testing facility—in a bag.

6. Label the bag with your name and place a brief note on it to indicate where the sample came from.

7. Fill out the test form and mail or deliver the samples. Do this immediately, in order to minimize changes in soil properties.

DIY COMPOSTING

Soil needs ongoing additions of organic matter to keep its flora and fauna happy. Without that, water infiltration, soil aeration, and porosity decrease—in short, not good for plants. The most effective amount of organic matter for optimal growth in the Pacific Northwest is between 4 and 10 percent organic matter by weight.

So if a soil test has shown your soil is short on organic matter, what's the best way to get more into it? Answer: compost. As you'll soon discover, this is a precious resource—it takes time, energy, and patience to make, but

Tuck a compost bin into the back of the garden and put your food scraps to work for you.

fortunately it doesn't have to cost much if you make it from your own kitchen leftovers and yard waste.

In fact, up to 20 percent of the solid waste that ends up in landfills comes from our yard waste. So instead of throwing organic matter in the trash or putting it in the yard waste bin for the city to pick up, use it at home. This will reduce unnecessary waste transport, which in turn lowers the production of methane gas. Plus, you won't have to drive to the garden store or soil factory to spend your hard-earned money on compost. You already have a valuable renewable resource right there in your perennial clippings and table scraps to build healthy soil and make an ideal environment for beneficial soil organisms.

The Science of Composting

To compost, you need decomposing organic debris, oxygen, water, and microorganisms and invertebrates (and the heat they create).

Bacteria, fungi, and actinomycetes (an intermediate organism between fungi and bacteria) are the primary decomposers and temperature raisers. Bacteria that require oxygen, called *aerobic bacteria*, provide the fastest and most effective composting. Insects, mites, millipedes, sowbugs, earthworms, and other organisms also help break up debris.

The amount of time it takes to convert organic material to compost depends on several key factors described below.

Aeration

More airflow means faster decomposition. Avoid letting compost materials get tightly compacted; constant turning of the material with a pitchfork or some other tool can better let fresh air in.

Moisture

The ideal compost pile is moist, like a wrung-out rag—not too dry and not too wet. If you pick up a handful of the material and squeeze it, it should feel damp and release just a drop or two of water. Too much water means too little oxygen, which encourages anaerobic bacteria to produce compounds that smell bad and harm plants. Too little water decreases the activity of the bacteria and slows decomposition.

Particle Size

The smaller the particle size, the greater the surface area exposed to air, and the faster the microorganisms will be able to decompose the material and generate heat. Thus, breaking or cutting up the material into smaller pieces will speed up the process.

Temperature

When microorganisms do their job, they generate heat. For the pile of organic material to heat up sufficiently, it needs to be the right size, which, from my experience, is roughly 1 cubic yard (3 feet by 3 feet by 3 feet). Smaller piles often don't heat up enough in the center, but at the same time letting the pile get any more than 5 feet high or wide runs the risk of cutting off the center of it from the oxygen supply.

The center of a 1 cubic yard pile will heat up to between 90°F and 140°F—optimal conditions for rapid composting. Temperatures of 130°F or greater will kill pathogens and weed seeds, but since this temperature is sometimes difficult to achieve in home composting, it is better to keep diseased material or weed seeds out of the compost pile in the first place. The most effective decomposing action of bacteria occurs at more moderate temperatures, between 70°F and 100°F. The temperature naturally varies throughout the process; after the first phase of high heat, the temperature tends to moderate itself.

Carbon-to-Nitrogen Ratio

Microorganisms use carbon and nitrogen from dead plants and animals to source energy and build protein. When the carbon-to-nitrogen (C:N) ratio is too high, meaning too little nitrogen, then the decomposition is slow. When the

LEFT: *Construct your compost bin to allow for maximum airflow.* **RIGHT:** *Finding the right balance between moisture and good drainage will result in perfect, loamy compost.*

ratio is too low, meaning too much nitrogen, then the bacteria can't digest it quickly enough and the pile off-gases nitrogen in the form of ammonia gas. If the C:N ratio of the mixture is in the range of 25:1 to 40:1, the composting process is reasonably efficient.

Composting 101

Building and maintaining a compost pile is simple, and the resulting rich material is well worth the wait.

Pick a Location

Moist compost is happy compost. Find a spot near a water source, so you can keep it moist during drier times, but the spot should have adequate drainage so that the pile won't get or stay too wet in the rain. If the pile becomes too wet, the anaerobic bacteria will begin decomposing the material; this process smells bad and produces compounds that can harm plants. For this reason, pick a location a safe distance from your living space, but close enough to be convenient. As for sun versus shade, a shaded area can keep the pile from drying out, but piles in full sun will compost faster, provided they are kept moist. Having the pile in partial shade is a good compromise.

Decide on Containers or Holding Units

Depending on the size of your space and your timeline, a single pile or holding unit may work just fine. Or you might want multiple piles or holding units to hold composting material at different stages of completion. There are many materials you can use to build your holding unit, each with its own pluses and minuses.

- **No container:** To keep it simple, just make a good-size, uncovered heap of yard waste about 3 feet high and 5 feet wide. I like this option, because piles on the ground are easiest to turn. To avoid attracting pests, place vegetable waste at the center.
- **Build your own:** Use galvanized chicken wire to create a circular wire-mesh holding unit, roughly 10 to 12 feet in circumference by 3 feet high and 3.5 feet wide, or about 1 cubic yard. This is simple and inexpensive to make and great for holding yard waste such as leaves. You can also use rot-resistant wood, wooden pallets, or snow fencing, all of which have spaces between the wood and fencing material to facilitate aeration. Add a lid to keep out raccoons and other pests. (See Resources for websites that offer guidance on building different types of compost bins.)
- **Buy a bin:** All you have to do is select a bin and place it in your garden.

Collect Materials

Stockpile enough yard waste and food scraps to make at least 1 cubic yard of material. If you have large chunks of material, chop things smaller, to a few inches, if you have the time and energy. The contents of the pile will get smaller as the material decomposes. Some materials may attract pests such as rats, dogs, or raccoons. Keep bones, meat, fish, dairy products, and all fatty foods, breads, sweets, and pet waste out of the compost pile.

Check Your Carbon:Nitrogen Levels

One of the best ways to create optimal conditions for organisms to do their work is to get your materials to the optimal C:N ratio of about 30:1. Start by blending different dry materials or bulking agents with a high C:N ratio. These include

- wood chips
- bark
- sawdust
- shredded paper
- hay or straw
- dead leaves

Then blend in material with a low ratio:

- green plant trimmings
- weeds without seeds and rhizomes (runners)
- vegetable and fruit scraps
- coffee grounds and tea bags
- cow, horse, or chicken manure (but not pet waste)

If you plan on using your compost on garden crops, it is OK to include fresh animal manure in your compost mixture, but don't add fresh manure directly to your vegetable plot because it can be contaminated by pathogens like *E. coli* and salmonella, and the high acidity of fresh manure can burn tender plants. Although grass clippings are an excellent source of nitrogen, it's best to leave them on the lawn, where they can provide nitrogen and other nutrients to the lawn itself.

Bonus: Mixing materials of different textures and sizes ensures better drainage.

Choose a Method

There are several ways to compost, depending on how much energy you want to expend.

Slow Composting

For those of you who don't expect to have the time or desire to get your hands dirty turning the compost, slow composting may be the most convenient approach. You will simply collect and mix your yard waste, then place it in a pile or holding unit for a year or so. You can mix it every few months, but with this method you will be freed from a schedule.

When the mixture turns dark and crumbly, your compost will be completely decomposed.

Fast Composting

The method for quickly turning yard waste into compost is more intensive but gets the job done fast. First, you want to be sure to have good air exposure, enough moisture, and a low C:N ratio in order for the material to break down quickly. To get this:

1. Add two parts bulking agent and one part energy material (see Check your Carbon:Nitrogen Levels, above, for a list of these materials) until you have a total of 1 cubic yard of material.
2. Mix thoroughly with a pitchfork. Make sure the mixture is moist but not soaking wet. If it's too wet, add more dry material and mix again.
3. Turn the material with a pitchfork as often as once a week, rotating material from the outside of the pile into the center and vice versa. This ensures that the mixture has good aeration and well-dispersed moisture.

Frequent mixing on a regular schedule greatly speeds up the composting process by providing the aerobic bacteria sufficient oxygen to break down the material. With this approach, the yard waste usually stays hot for several weeks, then cools down and reduces in volume, converting to compost in about two months. If you turn the material only once a month you slow the process somewhat, but it would still be considerably faster than just letting the mixture sit.

Water It

To determine whether your compost pile has that perfect damp-dishrag moistness, give a handful of the compost a squeeze. If it's too dry, add water and turn it. If it's too wet, add some dry material and turn it, thereby exposing it to the air to encourage drying. Cover

Regular use of compost and mulch holds in moisture and provides nutrients that helps a garden thrive.

the material during rainy weather for further moisture-accumulation prevention.

Let the Materials Cook

The rate at which the composting process occurs depends on the blend of materials, the temperature, and the amount of aeration and moisture. As long as the organisms doing the decomposing have the right diet and sufficient oxygen and water, they will get the job done.

Turn It

Turn the pile as frequently as desired, depending on which method you chose. Ideally, all material should get exposure to both the outside air and the inside of the pile. This not only makes for efficient composting but will produce higher temperatures that should kill pathogens and weed seeds—although, as noted previously, it is prudent in a home composting situation to leave out weeds that have gone to seed. The compost is done

A top-dressing of mulch around new plants (tall Oregon grape) reduces weed growth, helps keep the soil moist, reduces erosion, and protect plants from the cold.

when it's dark brown and crumbly, with a mild, earthy odor.

Dig In

The amount of compost to use in your soil depends on the purpose.

- Soil that's compacted or deficient in organic matter: Gently mix in 2–4 inches of high-quality, thoroughly cooked compost to a depth of 12 inches.
- Small perennials and herbaceous plants: Mix the compost into the soil down to 8 inches.
- Existing plants with a deficiency of organic matter: Add a top dressing of compost, 2 inches around annuals and perennials and

3–4 inches around woody shrubs and trees, but keep the compost a few inches away from the stem of the plant.

- After weeding: Top-dress with coarse compost on the soil surface after thorough weeding, regardless of whether the soil is compacted or deficient in organic matter.

MULCH

Mulch on top of compost is like frosting on the cake. Mulch is similar to compost in that it is usually a mixture of organic matter such as garden waste and fruit and vegetable scraps, but it differs in that it hasn't fully decomposed yet and so most of the plants are in their original form.

While a top dressing of mulch can be added any time of the year, early spring is probably the optimal time in the Northwest for most plants, as it helps keep the soil moist and prevents weed seedlings from sprouting. Fall is also an appropriate time to add mulch to protect plants from the cold, retard winter weeds, and reduce soil erosion.

On top of your newly composted soil, add a 2- to 4-inch layer of coarse organic mulch with a high C:N ratio, such as wood chips containing leaf fragments, to make a ground layer that will slowly decompose and add its benefits to the soil. This can hamper weed growth, buffer against compaction, and create microhabitats for plant seedlings and insects. Keep the mulch a few inches away from the stems of existing plants.

CHAPTER CHECKLIST

☐ Ideally the soil should be bustling with soil organisms to support healthy plants and provide habitat for plants and animals. Healthy soil is the foundation for a vibrant ecosystem and a sustainable, resilient garden.

☐ Get to know your soil by testing texture, pH, nutrients, and drainage.

☐ Improve drainage by mixing compost into the soil and/or installing underground drainage pipes.

☐ Make your own compost, and use mulch to improve soil structure and porosity; reduce bulk density and the need for irrigation and fertilizer; improve nutrient availability, plant growth, and disease resistance; increase water infiltration and water retention; enhance the binding and breakdown of pollutants in the soil; and improve habitat and provide nutrients for soil organisms.

4

TREES

As trees are the tallest and most dominant element in your landscape, usually live the longest, and are key to enhancing urban biodiversity, creating sustainable landscapes, and attracting urban wildlife, they are the most important plant choice in your yard. Therefore, particularly if you are working with an urban yard, consider their placement first before that of other plant material. Select a tree that is right for your location and site conditions, consistent with your overall goals for the garden, and that can perform the functions you deem important.

WHY TREES?

Urban trees, whether in private gardens, parks, woodlots, commercial or industrial areas, or along city streets, provide many environmental, economic, and social benefits to our gardens, neighborhoods, and communities. Trees enhance the quality of life in our cities just as they improve the aesthetics of urban streets—by softening the harsh visual impact of the dark impervious surfaces of roads and parking lots and by screening unsightly buildings, utility poles, and vacant lots. Trees do many things:

- Reduce stormwater flow and erosion by intercepting rain
- Cool the air by enhancing water evaporation from the surface of their leaves
- Take up water and break up tight soils through their extensive root systems, thereby boosting water infiltration

OPPOSITE: *A Chinese pistachio*, Pistacia chinensis, *shows off its dramatic fall colors.*

Street trees not only beautify neighborhoods, but they also perform other valuable functions in urban environments.

- Slow the rate at which water soaks into the soil, helping plant roots filter out pollutants
- Remove the greenhouse gas carbon dioxide during photosynthesis and store the carbon in their wood while releasing oxygen into the air—helping to reduce atmospheric carbon dioxide and provide a sink for carbon storage
- Moderate heat and wind such that energy needed for heating and cooling is reduced, thereby lowering the amount of burned fossil fuels
- Provide food and shelter for pollinators and other beneficial wildlife, and enhance the richness and biodiversity of bird species
- Make canopies with their overarching branches in neighborhoods and downtown business districts, creating an aesthetically pleasing and calming environment and habitat for birds and other wildlife
- Help create a sense of local identity and community, and inspire environmental stewardship
- Increase property value

HOW TO CHOOSE A TREE FOR YOUR YARD

The first question to ask yourself is why you want to plant a tree. Do you want it for a screen to provide privacy or block a view of the neighbors? While evergreen trees don't make good shade trees, they can make effective screens. They are also superior to deciduous trees for slowing stormwater runoff (rainfall that flows over the surface of the ground). Evergreens help decrease the amount of pollutants reaching local waters, because even in winter their leaves absorb rain. If you select an evergreen tree to serve as a screen, make sure its mature size will not be too large for the site.

How about shade? You may want to shade your home in the summer with a deciduous tree on the south or west side. This would make the house cooler in summer and reduce your use of air-conditioning. And while you're at it, do you want light shade, dappled shade, or heavy shade? Do you want to shade your patio or deck? If so, consider whether a particular tree will drop seedpods or other debris. All these aspects need consideration when you're selecting trees.

Next consider the visual element. Do you want an evergreen with leaves or needles that persist all year, or a deciduous tree that loses its leaves every fall? Attractive flowering trees, such as dogwood or crab apple, can add beauty to your yard. Would you like the tree to flower in spring or summer? What color flowers do you prefer? Do you want it to attract more birds to your property? You might also consider growing a fruit tree for your family.

You must also determine whether a tree you have in mind is right for the site conditions

A deciduous tree on the south side of a house creates shade and cools the house in summer and allows warming light into the house in winter.

Choose trees carefully to ensure you don't create problems down the line, such as buckled sidewalks and hardscapes.

and air quality, enhancing wildlife habitat, and enhancing your health and well-being. To help you get started, see Trees for All Seasons, later in this chapter.

NATIVE OR NONNATIVE?

Whether or not you choose trees—and, more broadly, plants—native to the Pacific Northwest depends on many factors. Below are some factors to take into consideration when deciding between native and nonnative plants; each can have a place and purpose in your garden.

Native Species

A native species grows in a particular region, ecosystem, or habitat without direct or indirect human action. For example, "species native to North America" generally refers to those species that were present on the North American continent before the arrival of European settlers. So, why would we want to have native plants in our gardens?

- They are the lifeblood of a healthy ecosystem, since they provide food, shelter, water, and living space to native creatures above and below ground.
- They are naturally adapted to the local climate and soil conditions, unless the soil

and the soil. Select one that is suitable for your climate and the specific microclimate in your yard, including sun exposure and drainage. Make sure that the expected height and width at maturity will fit the available space. Will there be adequate space for the roots? Will the roots be far enough from the driveway, patio, or any utility lines or pipes to avoid causing damage? Select a tree that grows moderately; fast-growing trees usually do not live long, and their limbs tend to be weak and brittle and more prone to breaking than slower-growing trees. You also want the tree to be low maintenance, pest and disease resistant, and drought tolerant.

Make sure that the tree fits your overall goals for the site and will contribute to sustainable landscape practices: conserving water and energy, helping protect water

Nonnative trees such as Chinese dogwoods, Cornus kousa 'Heart Throb' (pink) in front and Cornus kousa 'National' (white) in back (left) and handkerchief tree, Davidia involucrate (right), can work well in Pacific Northwest gardens.

has been significantly disturbed, and are therefore easy to grow and maintain.

- They attract an array of beneficial predators and parasites that keep harmful insects in check.
- They are sensitive to pollution and other harmful conditions of urban environments; the state of their health can signify, like the proverbial canary in the coal mine, the health of the surrounding area.
- They bring nature's beauty—including birds and butterflies and other insects—to your doorstep.
- They provide a sense of regional identity.

Nonnative Species

Nonnative, or introduced, species are those that have put down roots outside their original range, in an environment where they do not naturally occur. Human activity is usually to blame: people, accidently or deliberately, transport nonnative species to the new location.

So why would we want to have nonnative plants in our gardens?

- They are often more adaptable to urban environments than native plants.
- They fill ecological niches that natives once filled, after ecosystem damage has caused the natives to fail.
- They serve as "nurse plants" by modifying harsh conditions and thereby facilitating the eventual return of native species.
- They provide shelter, nesting sites, and food to native animals.
- They add new and interesting textures, forms, colors, and scents to local gardens.
- They supply vegetables, fruits, and nuts.

SCIENCE-BASED PLANTING

As trees are generally the most expensive specimens in the garden, take great care to

plant them properly. The procedure for planting trees varies with the production method used in the nursery. There are three main types of production methods for nursery trees: *balled-and-burlapped*, *container-grown*, and *bare root*. Following is what you need to know about them.

Balled-and-Burlapped

Balled-and-burlapped (B&B) is the most common method for transplanting large trees. A significant advantage to this method is that, although B&B trees usually have more than 90 percent of their root systems removed, they can be stored and planted throughout the growing season and generally have high transplant survival rates. However, having the burlap or basket comes with some cons, one of which is that, if the roots are covered, then you can't see root defects or problematic soil. You'll need to identify suppliers, through experience or the recommendations of others, that can provide high-quality B&B trees without root defects or lots of soil over the root collar. The trees should also have been grown in soil with a similar texture to the soil at your planting site. If this is not possible, consider buying bare root or container-grown trees.

How to Plant

1. Locate and expose the trunk flare—where the trunk begins to spread out as it meets the roots—by removing the

TOP: *Measure the root ball of your balled-and-burlapped tree and dig the planting hole to the same depth.*
BOTTOM: *Once you've placed the tree, the trunk flare should be slightly above the surrounding ground.*

top portion of the burlap and soil from the top of the root ball.

2. Dig the planting hole no deeper than the root ball as measured from the trunk flare to the bottom of the root ball. Make the hole in shape of a bowl, with the top three times the diameter of the root ball and the bottom about two times the diameter of the root ball. To prevent the root ball from settling in the hole after planting, it is essential that the soil in the bottom of the hole remain undisturbed and firm.

3. Move the tree by holding the root ball rather than the trunk of the tree. Set the tree in the hole so that the trunk flare or top of the root mass will be about 2 inches above the finished grade (the top surface of the soil area around the backfill).

4. Carefully cut away the twine, and remove as much of the wire and burlap as possible without breaking up the root ball. Inspect the root ball for circling or hooked roots and remove them with a sharp pruner.

5. Backfill the hole with the dug-up (native) soil by gently packing soil around the base of the root ball to stabilize it. Water thoroughly after the planting hole is half-full. Then completely backfill the hole but leave the trunk flare completely exposed.

6. Build a small berm with leftover backfill around the tree a few feet from the trunk to keep the water near the roots of the tree. You should remove the berm once the tree is established.

7. Water the tree thoroughly to saturate the soil and remove air pockets.

8. Place 3 inches of organic mulch on top of the surface around the tree, about three times the diameter of the root ball, while keeping the mulch a few inches away from the tree collar.

9. If the tree is unable to stand upright on its own, stake the tree low and loose with two stakes and separate flexible, nonabrasive ties for no longer than 1 year. Trees staked too tightly or for more than 1 year will be weak and subject to breakage.

An alternative way to plant B&B trees is to remove the soil from the root ball prior to planting, which eliminates any differences in soil texture and permits you to more thoroughly inspect and remove defective roots. Plant as described for bare root trees, below.

The downside of this approach is that you must plant in late fall or early spring when the tree is still dormant, in order to avoid transplant shock, which can kill the tree; even when transplanted well, some B&B trees cannot withstand the shock of bare root planting.

Container-Grown

Trees produced in containers have the major advantage of allowing all the roots to be moved with the transplant, thus greatly

When you buy a containerized plant such as this star magnolia (top), you may need to prune the girdling, kinked, and hooked roots (top right). When planting, set on a firm mound in the center of the planting hole and spread the roots radially and horizontally (bottom right).

minimizing transplant shock, particularly if they are planted during the growing season. Container-grown trees are also lighter and therefore easier to handle and ship than B&B trees.

However, containerized plants can be planted too deep at the nursery, covering the root collar with soil and causing serious defects in their roots, such as kinking, hooking, or girdling. Purchase only healthy, high-quality nursery stock that has a root collar at the container's surface. The porous potting mix will initially have more nutrients and oxygen and a different texture than the planting site's soil, differences that will cause water to drain away from the roots and make it difficult for them to establish. Therefore, it is usually better to remove the container media and save it to use as a top dressing.

How to Plant

1. Dig the planting hole as deep as the root mass and two to three times its diameter.

2. Remove the container media and the soil surrounding the roots.

3. Inspect the roots for defects and correct them by straightening out the roots or pruning off the portion of the roots that are kinked, hooked, or girdling.

4. Gently set the tree on a firm mound in the center of the planting hole, spreading the roots radially and horizontally.

5. Make sure that the trunk flare or top of the root mass is slightly (about 2 inches) above the surrounding grade.

6. Backfill with native soil.

7. Spread the leftover container media and soil around the base of the tree.

8. Water until the entire backfill material is moist.

9. Stake the tree low and loose with two stakes and separate flexible ties for no longer than 1 year.

Bare Root

Bare root trees are an excellent alternative to B&B or containerized trees. They are much less expensive to purchase and transport, and are lighter and easier to handle than trees produced by other production methods. Also, they contain considerably more of their original roots than B&B trees. Furthermore, all the roots and the root collar (trunk flare) are visible when you purchase the tree. Bare root plants are generally smaller (the diameter of the trunk is usually less than 2 inches) than those obtained by other production methods; however, it takes smaller trees less time

TOP: *Top-dress a newly planted tree with mulch but keep the mulch away from the trunk.* **BOTTOM:** *Correct staking of a new tree*

LEFT: *After cutting off the end of the branch you want to remove, prune the remaining branch at the branch collar.*
RIGHT: *After pruning, the branch collar remains.*

to replace their roots, and such trees generally get established more quickly than larger ones.

Bare root trees are harvested dormant and are therefore available for planting only in early spring or late fall. The choice of size and species available may be limited. It is critical that their roots stay moist during shipping, handling, and planting, so have the nursery dip them in a gel-slurry and place them in a large plastic bag just prior to transport. Bare root plantings can be just as successful as B&B plantings if given careful attention and maintenance to ensure that the roots do not dry out.

How to Plant

1. Inspect the roots. If the roots are circling or hooked, straighten them out if you can; if not, cut them off with a sharp pruner.
2. Dig the hole as deep as the root system and twice as wide.
3. Firm up a central soil mound and arrange the roots radially around it so that the trunk flare is about 2 inches above the existing grade.
4. Backfill with native soil and gently firm the soil.
5. Water until the entire backfill is moist.
6. Mulch the planting area with 3 inches of mulch, but keep the mulch away from the tree collar.
7. Stake the tree low and loose with two stakes and separate flexible ties for no longer than 1 year.

TREE MAINTENANCE AND PRUNING

Trees should be maintained and protected from damage throughout their lives to maximize their health and benefits. As a tree grows, its value and benefits to the garden and neighborhood increase substantially. Maintain a mulched, grass-free area around a tree so that you avoid damaging its trunk or bark with a weed trimmer or lawnmower. To protect the roots, avoid trenching or placing paved sidewalk or driveway within the critical root zone of the tree—approximate the critical root zone by determining the outside edge of the canopy, called the drip line. Avoid driving over the critical root zone with a car or heavy equipment. Avoid removing or adding soil around the base of a tree within the critical root zone.

Most ornamental trees need only minimal pruning to stay healthy and vigorous. If you selected trees that, at their mature size, will fit the space available, you won't have to prune in excess later on. But if you find dead, diseased, or damaged branches, it is important to remove them in a timely fashion to keep the plant healthy, and this does wonders for the overall appearance of the garden. Cut back to healthy tissue, as indicated by a thin layer of green tissue or *cambium* just beneath the bark. It is best to make the cut on a dry day; use a sharp pruner that you have cleaned and disinfected first with something like Lysol to minimize the transfer of disease organisms, particularly if you have been pruning diseased plants with the same pruner. Cut back to a branch collar (the distinctive bulge or swollen area at the base of the branch) or bud to give the plant a balanced and natural look. If suckers appear at the base of a plant, rub them off by hand—rather than cutting them—as soon as they appear.

For deciduous trees and shrubs, summer is a good time to prune out deadwood

A poorly pruned tree will never regain its natural form.

because the deadwood will have either no leaves or dead leaves and thus be easy to recognize. Tree varieties that flower between early spring and mid-June can be pruned immediately after flowering. Varieties that bloom between mid-June and fall should be pruned in winter. Avoid late summer or early fall pruning, as the new growth that occurs in response to pruning is not likely to have time to harden off before a hard frost occurs. This can seriously damage new growth. Winter, after the woody plant has reached full dormancy (the period when it is no longer growing), is a good time to prune, provided the weather is dry and above freezing. Most evergreen trees are pruned at the end of winter.

DEFINING LIGHT REQUIREMENTS FOR PLANTS

In specifying light requirements, I use the following definitions:

- *Full sun:* More than 6 hours of direct sunlight per day, especially in the afternoon.
- *Partial sun:* Four to 6 hours of direct sunlight per day, with the majority of the sunlight coming in the afternoon.
- *Partial shade:* Three to 6 hours of sunlight per day, with most of the sunlight coming in the morning or early afternoon, or dappled shade with sunlight filtering through the canopy of deciduous trees or lattice structures regardless of the time of day.
- *Full shade:* Permanent shade throughout the day, cast by the shadows of trees, buildings, walls, or hedges, with little direct sunlight.

While thinning a tree can open up the canopy, reduce wind resistance, improve air circulation, and allow light to penetrate, whenever possible allow trees and shrubs to maintain their natural shape, branch structure, and growth characteristics. Never cut a tree's top off to reduce a tree's size. Instead, thin the branches evenly throughout the canopy or cut tall branches back to shorter, large-diameter side branches to reduce foliage. Take care to remove less than 25 percent of the total leaf area.

Other techniques include *winnowing*, selectively removing a limb, and *skirting*, removing lower limbs. Be sure to keep at least two-thirds of the limbs intact, no matter the method. Avoid making unnecessary shearing cuts unless you're going for one of those straight-rowed or funny-shaped formal hedges, in which case you should thin on last year's growth, or "old wood." Careful pruning when the tree is still young can help promote a straight trunk, improve structure, and minimize the need for significant pruning when the tree is mature.

TREES FOR ALL SEASONS

Trees are your biggest investment in the landscape, generally live longer than shrubs and perennials, and can provide the greatest environmental benefits. The list of trees in this chapter includes a mix of native and nonnative ornamentals that are generally drought tolerant. Any one of them would be an excellent choice for an urban yard in need of additional beauty, shade, wildlife habitat, or screening. Each entry lists the tree's mature size, light requirements, soil preferences, pollinators, and USDA (see map in Chapter 2, Assessing Your Yard) and Sunset zones, which are widely used zones defined in *The New Western Garden Book* by the editors of *Sunset* magazine (see Resources).

Native Ornamental Trees

Northwest native plants, adapted to our soils and climate, play a vital role in the natural web of life. Our native birds, mammals, amphibians, and insects are dependent on these indigenous plants; therefore, it is important that each of us incorporate more native plants into our gardens.

CASCARA

Frangula purshiana

A small deciduous tree, cascara has small greenish-yellow flowers and purplish-black, bird-friendly fruit.

Mature size: 18–34 ft. tall x 9–17 ft. wide

Light requirement: Sun to partial shade

Soil: Moist, well draining

Pollinators: Bees

USDA zone: 4–9

Sunset zone: 1–9, 14–17

Other: Drought tolerant, shade tolerant

MOUNTAIN HEMLOCK

Tsuga mertensiana

This small evergreen grows slowly into a slender, conical shape, with the central leader drooping at the top, a common characteristic of hemlocks. A native of the mountains of the American West, it is densely covered by green or blue-green needles. Once established, it does not require maintenance.

Mature size: 20–30 ft. tall x 9–14 ft. wide

Light requiement: Full sun to partial shade

Soil: Tolerates variable soils; prefers cool, moist, loose, coarse-textured (sandy), well-draining soil.

Pollinators: Wind

USDA zone: 5–9

Pacific dogwood, Cornus nattallii

Sunset zone: A1–A3; 1–7, 14–17

Other: Tolerates severe weather, dry, windy sites, and drought. However, it does not tolerate pollution, extreme heat, poor circulation, or nitrogen-containing fertilizers.

PACIFIC DOGWOOD

Cornus nuttallii

This attractive, small, flowering deciduous tree has small greenish flowers and showy creamy-white bracts in spring followed by clusters of red berries.

Mature size: 28–48 ft. tall x 14–24 ft. wide

Light requirement: Partial shade

Soil: Moist, well draining, and acidic

Pollinators: Bees, beetles, flies, butterflies

USDA zone: 7–9

Sunset zone: 3b–9, 14–20

Other: Drought tolerant

PACIFIC MADRONE

Arbutus menziesii

A particularly striking, picturesque broad-leaved evergreen tree with cinnamon-brown to red peeling bark, the madrone has creamy-white flowers and small red fruits. Unfortunately, it is prone to fungal disease, so it's important to site this tree in well-draining soil in full sun with good air circulation.

Pacific madrone, Arbutus menziesii

Mature size: 30–75 ft. tall x 18–35 ft. wide

Light requirement: Full sun

Soil: Dry, well draining

Pollinators: Bees, hummingbirds

USDA zone: 7–9

Sunset zone: 4–7, 14–19

Other: Prefers south-, west-, or southwest-facing slopes. Drought and salt spray tolerant.

PACIFIC SERVICEBERRY

Amelanchier alnifolia

An adaptable deciduous shrub or small multi-trunked tree having clusters of white, fragrant five-petaled flowers in spring followed by blue berrylike fruit. The spring leaves tend toward purple, then turn green in summer and fiery scarlet hues in fall.

Mature size: 10–15 ft. tall and wide

Light requirement: Full sun to partial shade

Soil: Dry or moist, well draining; tolerates many soil types.

Pollinators: Bees, flies, butterflies, hummingbirds

USDA zone: 2–9

Sunset zone: A1–A3; 1–6

Other: Drought tolerant; flowers attract pest-eating insects, fruit is relished by birds and mammals.

VINE MAPLE

Acer circinatum

This adaptable deciduous shrub or small tree has a moderate growth rate. In the spring, the new leaves emerge red, along with small clusters of white-petaled flowers. The leaves turn a pale to yellowish green during the summer and by fall change to shades of red and gold. The bark starts out green but gradually turns reddish brown with age.

Mature size: 15–25 ft. tall and wide

The emerging delicate flowers and leaves of vine maple, Acer circinatum

Light requirements: Partial sun to partial shade; its leaves burn if exposed to afternoon sun. Under sunny conditions, it tends to have a single trunk, but in shade it is more likely to form a multistemmed clump.

Soil: Prefers acidic, well-draining soil.

Pollinators: Bees (mason, bumble); host plant for the western tiger swallowtail butterfly.

USDA zone: 5–9

Sunset zone: A3; 2b–6, 14–17

Other: Vine maples are great as understory for the urban garden.

Nonnative Ornamental Trees

In this section, I have compiled information about eleven nonnative trees that are not commonly grown in Northwest gardens; each of them, however, has unique and special qualities that merit consideration for growing in the Northwest. They are all growing and healthy in my garden and hardy in USDA zones 7 or less. None of them had any problem in the fall of 2010 when my garden experienced temperatures of 15°F to 20°F for days along with high winds up to 50 miles per hour in early November before the trees had time to become dormant. Perhaps you will have a place for one or more of these fine trees in your garden.

AMUR MAACKIA

Maackia amurensis

A small and adaptable shade tree, the Amur maackia grows slowly, about 12 feet per 20

years. It is round or vase shaped, with peeling and shiny coppery-brown bark and silvery unfolding buds in spring. Before the 1- to 3-inch long seedpods develop, the clusters of slightly fragrant, creamy-white flowers attract bees come summer. As a member of the pea plant family (Fabaceae) it is one of the few trees that support nitrogen-fixing bacteria in their roots. An excellent residential shade tree, it can be planted near a patio or deck; its adaptability also makes it suitable for planting next to a street.

Mature size: 20–30 ft. tall and wide

Light requirement: Full sun

Soil: Prefers loose, well-draining soil but tolerates a wide range of soil conditions, including heavy clay, acidity, or alkalinity. Does not tolerate salt spray or soils with high salts.

Pollinators: Bees

USDA zone: 6–9

Sunset zone: 1–10, 14–17

Other: Tolerates drought and cold. Requires minimal maintenance if given proper cultural conditions.

CEDAR OF LEBANON 'GREEN PRINCE'

Cedrus libani 'Green Prince'

The dwarf seedling 'Green Prince' is a specialty of Wells Nursery in Mount Vernon, Washington, but is now available at other nurseries that specialize in conifers. It grows slowly, at about 3–4 inches per year, into a picturesque evergreen with a single trunk, many spirally arranged horizontal branches, and stiff, dark green needles. Cone shaped when young, this tree eventually broadens after many years, forming a flat-topped crown. Using the wind as a conduit, the lower male pollen-containing yellow-brown cones pollinate the upper female purplish to brown cones. This species originates from the Mediterranean region, particularly Lebanon and Turkey.

Mature size: 15–20 ft. tall and wide

Light requirement: Full sun

Soil: Tolerates sandy or clay loam and prefers moist, well-draining soil.

Pollinators: Wind

USDA zone: 6–9

Sunset zone: 3–10, 14–24

Other: Once established, it is drought tolerant and requires minimal maintenance.

CHINESE PISTACHIO

Pistacia chinensis

An excellent medium-growing deciduous shade tree from China, the Chinese pistachio is adaptable to urban areas and usually pest free. It has lustrous dark green compound leaves in spring and summer that turn fiery orange and red in fall. Female trees produce red berries attractive to birds, while the flowers attract a variety of insects.

Mature size: 40–50 ft. tall x 35 ft. wide

Light requirement: Full sun

Soil: Must be well draining, otherwise adaptable to sandy and clay soils and a range of soil pH.

Cedar of Lebanon, Cedrus labani *'Green Prince'*

Chinese pistachio, Pistacia chinensis

Pollinators: Wind
USDA zone: 6–9
Sunset zone: 4–7, 16 and 17 (warmer parts), 18–23
Other: Tolerates drought, heat, and wind.

DOVE OR HANDKERCHIEF TREE

Davidia involucrata

Sometimes known as the ghost tree, this deciduous tree is native to China. It was named for its flowers: small, reddish-purple flower heads surrounded by a pair of large, unequal, papery white bracts. These flowers tend to flutter in the breeze, resembling doves or handkerchiefs. The flowers are followed by green nuts that become purple when ripe.

Mature size: 40 ft. tall x 35 ft. wide
Light requirement: Full sun to partial shade
Soil: Prefers fertile, moist, well-draining soils.
Pollinators: Bees, beetles
USDA zone: 6–8
Sunset zone: 4–9, 14–21
Other: Place in a sheltered position that is protected from strong winds. Unselected species may take a dozen years or more before flowering. For this reason, I recommend a cultivar called 'Sonoma' that can bloom the first year it is planted. It grows moderately fast and requires supplemental water during long dry periods typical of summers in the Northwest.

JUDAS TREE

Cercis siliquastrum

This bushy deciduous tree from southern Europe and west Asia blooms rosy-pink to white pea-shaped flowers on old wood, including the trunk, in late spring before the heart-shaped leaves sprout. It subsequently produces long, flat vertical seedpods.

Mature size: 30 ft. tall and wide
Light requirement: Full sun to partial shade
Soil: Deep, well draining
Pollinators: Bees
USDA zone: 6–9
Sunset zone: 3b–19
Other: Drought tolerant

OYAMA MAGNOLIA

Magnolia sieboldii

This vase-shaped, deciduous large shrub or small tree is native to woodland areas of eastern Asia. Branch tips bear drooping, fragrant, cup-shaped white flowers accented with crimson stamens from late May to July. After blooming, pink oval seedpods are formed. By autumn, the green leaves turn golden yellow.

Judas tree, Cercis siliquastrum

Oyama magnolia, Magnolia sieboldii

Mature size: 15–25 ft. tall and wide

Light requirement: Partial shade; in the maritime Northwest, where there are cool summers, it can be grown in full sun.

Soil: Moist, rich, acidic, well-draining soils

Pollinators: Bees

USDA zone: 6–9

Sunset zone: 4–9, 14–24

Other: Place mulch on the roots to help retain moisture and water during dry periods.

PERSIAN IRONWOOD

Parrotia persica

Native to Iran, this deciduous tree forms a rounded multitrunk with peeling bark, tends to be pest and disease free, and has year-round appeal. For me, Persian ironwood's best qualities are its relatively large, oval-shaped leaves, which unfold reddish purple and greenish edged, then mature to a lustrous green. As early as late July, they begin displaying various fall hues of bronze, burnt orange, yellow, and crimson, retaining this kaleidoscope of colors until the leaves drop in November. In February and early March, small red flowers with a profusion of spidery-looking crimson stamens appear before the leaves. This tough, durable, long-lived, and drought-tolerant tree is an excellent tree for the garden or street.

Mature size: 25–40 ft. tall x 20–35 ft. wide

Light requirement: Full sun to partial shade

Soil: Does well in sandy or clay soil that is acidic or slightly alkaline; however, the soil should be well draining.

Pollinators: Wind

USDA zone: 5–8

Sunset zone: 2b–7, 14–17

Other: I prefer to grow two selected cultivars of Persian ironwood, 'Vanessa' and 'Pendula'. 'Vanessa' tends to be columnar with an ultimate height of 40 ft. and a spread of about 20 ft., while 'Pendula' is low spreading, reaching no more than 10–12 ft. high but ultimately spreading to 30–35 ft. wide.

SOURWOOD

Oxydendrum arboreum

Sourwood is a slow-growing, narrow, tall deciduous tree with a slender, usually leaning, trunk. Sprays of small white bell-

Persian ironwood, Parrotia persica

Sourwood, Oxydendrum arboreum

shaped, fragrant, nectar-rich flowers appear in summer. By autumn, drooping strands of berries develop and the smooth green leaves turn to bright crimson with tints of gold and purple. It's native to the east coast of North America but is quite adaptable to our Pacific Northwest climate.

Mature size: 25–35 ft. tall x 12–20 ft. wide

Light requirement: Full to partial sun

Soil: Prefers moist, acidic, well-draining sandy loam; dislikes heavy clay soils.

Pollinators: Bees, butterflies, moths

USDA zone: 5–9

Sunset zone: 2b–9, 14–17

Other: Incorporation of compost throughout the root zone helps lighten heavy soil, if you have it, and improve drainage. Sourwood will not thrive if its roots have competition from other plants growing underneath it. Therefore, remove all plants or lawn from the tree's root zone and replace with a thick layer of mulch; don't plant underneath it. To keep the roots moist, water during periods of drought.

ORANGE BARK STEWARTIA

Stewartia monadelpha

Orange Bark Stewartia is a small deciduous tree with four-season interest. It grows slowly and has flaking tan-orange bark, and the dark green leaves turn orange and red in the fall. Small, white cupped flowers similar to camellias appear in June.

Mature size: 20–25 ft. tall x 15–20 ft. wide

Light requirement: Full sun to partial shade

Soil: Needs moist, well-draining, acidic to neutral soil containing an ample supply of organic matter.

Pollinators: Bees

USDA zone: 6–8

Sunset zone: 4–6, 14–17, 20–21

Other: An occasional deep watering during an extended dry spell is beneficial. Shade the roots with groundcovers and/or mulch to prevent the roots from drying out.

THREE FLOWER MAPLE

Acer triflorum

Bright new leaves emerge from dark brown buds in spring. Soon thereafter, this small deciduous tree grows rather inconspicuous greenish-yellow flowers in clusters of three, followed by the winged seeds (samaras) typical of maples. Its orange-brown bark peels in long vertical strips. The green leaves turn shades of red, apricot, and yellow in fall.

Mature size: 20–30 ft. tall and wide

Light requirement: Partial sun to light shade

Soil: Prefers moist, acidic, well-draining soil; tolerates sandy and clay soils, but is intolerant of poor drainage and alkaline soils.

Pollinators: Bees

USDA zone: 5–8

Sunset zone: Not available

Other: This durable, moderately drought-tolerant tree can be used in the garden and as a residential street tree.

WHITEBEAM

Sorbus aria 'Lutescens'

Whitebeam is a small- to medium-size tree native to Europe and Great Britain. It has

Whitebeam, Sorbus aria 'Lutescens'

a symmetrical crown, with whitish-green leaves covered by small silver hairs and a profusion of fragrant white flower clusters. The flowers develop into bunches of red berries that are particularly attractive to birds. By fall, the leaves become yellowish brown and drop early.

Mature size: 25–40 ft. tall x 20–30 ft. wide

Light requirement: Full sun to partial shade

Soil: Tolerates dry or acid soils but not poor-draining soils; grows best in alkaline soils.

Pollinators: Bees

USDA zone: 5–9

Sunset zone: 3–10, 14–17

Other: This durable and nearly maintenance-free tree is adaptable to a garden, park, or street and tolerates heat, wind, maritime exposure, and pollution.

NONNATIVE FRUIT AND NUT TREES

Many fruit and nut tree varieties thrive in Pacific Northwest backyards. Filberts (hazelnuts), walnuts, and chestnuts do well in some regions, particularly in the Willamette Valley, southern Oregon, and the Oregon coastal region 15 to 20 miles inland, but can also be grown in many areas of Western Washington. Some filberts, walnuts, and chestnuts can be grown in the warmer regions east of the Cascades. Nut trees should be grown in a sunny location with well-draining soil.

Filberts require two different varieties with similar flowering periods for pollination. Space them 15–20 feet apart. Walnuts are self-fertile, but may produce walnuts at a younger age if a second variety is planted. Black walnuts are spaced 30–40 feet apart while English walnuts are spaced 40–50 feet apart. Chinese, European, and American chestnuts and their hybrids can be grown in the Northwest, but it is important to plant blight-resistant varieties. To insure pollination, plant two different varieties. For maximum long-term production, space chestnut trees 40 feet or more apart. To increase nut production over the first 20 years, space the trees about 20 feet apart and then eventually remove trees that become too close to each other.

Most regions—if you exclude areas directly along the coast with high rainfall, lots of fog, windy conditions, and generally milder summer and winter temperatures—can grow a large variety of fruit trees. The fruit varieties that ripen early, such as apples, Asian pears, cherries, and plums, are generally best for the cooler regions of the Pacific Northwest, while the interior portions of Western Washington and Oregon from Longview, Washington, to Roseburg, Oregon, can grow fruits that take longer to ripen, including apricots, figs, kiwis, peaches, and persimmons.

If deer are known to roam in your area, have a plan to keep them away from your trees; they love young fruit trees. It may be as simple as having a watchdog who loves to chase deer away, or it may require putting up an 8-foot deer fence. Many varieties of fruit trees either require another variety nearby to provide pollen or grow more fruit when a pollinator is nearby.

Plant your fruit trees in a well-drained, warm, sunny location that gets at least 8 hours of sun each day, such as an open, gentle south-facing slope. Space them based on the expected mature height of the tree. Thus, standard apple trees that get 30 feet tall should be spaced 30 feet apart, semidwarf trees that get about 16 feet high would be spaced 16 feet apart, and dwarf trees that grow to 8 feet can be spaced 8 feet apart. Fruit trees generally require annual pruning to maintain health; improve airflow, light penetration, and natural form; and increase fruit production. The best time to prune is when the trees are dormant, between late November and early March. Alternatively, they can be pruned in late July or early August. Prune cherries in summer to minimize bacterial canker.

CHAPTER CHECKLIST

☐ Select trees that match your site conditions and provide beauty and functionality.

☐ To better ensure long, healthy lives for your trees, take great care to follow science-based planting procedures for each of the main types of nursery production methods: bare root, container-grown, and B&B.

☐ Properly maintain your valuable tree and protect it from damage to maximize its benefits to you and the environment.

5

ORNAMENTALS
AND EDIBLES

Most of us wouldn't get married without considerable thought and research (otherwise known as dating). Use the same amount of consideration in matching a plant and a microclimate as you would before asking someone to spend a romantic week with you in Baja—don't just run to the garden store and fill your cart with any old plant.

When selecting plants, you should aim to enhance a site's beauty, resiliency, and biodiversity. Since you'll be investing considerable time and effort (and likely money), you'll want to go into the process with as much knowledge as possible. If you grow a plant in the appropriate site conditions, it should flourish in your garden with minimal care.

PLANNING FOR PLANTS

The first step is to consider how you want to use your landscape and the characteristics of the site (consult the site map you created in Chapter 2, Assessing Your Yard), and the plants' intended functions. If you have a small yard in the heart of Portland that receives mostly sun, you might want groundcovers to suppress weeds, a small planter box of annual vegetables or herbs, and a less time- and resource-intensive lawn. In a typically shady front yard, you may desire low-maintentance shrubs and perennials that will add beauty year-round.

OPPOSITE: *Blueberries are easy and rewarding to grow in the Pacific Northwest.*

LEFT: *These new shrubs are spaced sufficiently apart to allow the plants to grow to maturity without significant competition.* RIGHT: *This small seedling will someday be as large as the tree in the background.*

You must also know the available space for the plants above- and belowground. Although some mature woody plants have root zones not much bigger than the canopy, roots of some shrubs can extend two to four times the width of the canopy. So avoid planting them near utility lines or water pipes. Plan ahead for how much space a plant will eventually fill and give it adequate growing space. A friend of mine bought a house in the early spring, and by the time June rolled around, all the plants had filled out to their most robust state and were smothering one another. The previous owner told her that he had planted all his little sprouts right next to each other, hoping to create a lush urban jungle as quickly as possible. Seven years later, my friend had to cut down twelve trees so that the others would have room to grow. So don't overdo it.

Next consider the plants' compatibility with their intended microclimate, including the soil characteristics, precipitation patterns, exposure to drought or flooding conditions, and exposure to sun and wind (see the plant lists later in this chapter). Plan to group plantings of each species/cultivar rather than as single plants, and group plants by growth rate.

Strive to obtain locally propagated, produced, and sourced plants and seeds. In general, it is a good rule of thumb to select plants adapted to the local climate. For example, if a plant is not adapted to the wet winters and dry summers typical of the Northwest, it is more likely to become unhealthy and be more vulnerable to pests and diseases. Likewise, research a plant's geographic origin and native microclimate. While matching natives to their specific microclimates is a good place to start, you can also find suitable nonnatives from other regions whose climate and soil requirements are suited to your site.

Consider the plant's unique qualities, such as its flowers, fruits, scents, and colors; how it changes through the seasons; and whether it is pest and disease resistant, tolerates salt spray, withstands very dry summers without supplemental water, requires good drainage, or thrives in heavy clay soils. Include plants that provide food, shelter, and nesting sites for native animals.

When selecting plants, look at the assessment you made in Chapter 2 of your site's microclimates and soil, and ask yourself these questions:

- Do the plant's needs fit the resources of its intended microclimate?
- Is it similar to other plants in the community, and therefore able to thrive within the same climate?
- Will the plant fulfill its desired functions in the landscape, such as providing shade, serving as an ornamental accent, or acting as a groundcover to help suppress weeds?
- Will it contribute interest to the garden throughout the seasons and years?
- Do you know for certain that the plant is not overly aggressive?
- Does the plant have minimal maintenance requirements?
- Will the plant enhance biodiversity? Will it attract beneficial organisms or predators of pests? Can it support the needs of wildlife?

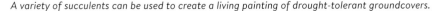

A variety of succulents can be used to create a living painting of drought-tolerant groundcovers.

- Will the plant contribute to the site's plant diversity?
- Does the plant reflect local character?
- Will the plant fit into the space available when it reaches maturity?

If you can answer yes to all these questions, then you certainly should have a gem that is worth planting. Not all plants will have all of these desirable qualities, however, and for some the answers may not all be clear. Ideally, you want to select long-lived and functional plants that thrive with minimal inputs of water, fertilizer, pruning, or other maintenance needs, and are compatible with your specific site. Avoid aggressive or invasive plants that can outcompete their neighbors or damage habitat for native plants and animals.

MULTILAYERED LANDSCAPES

As you choose trees to plant, consider how you will create layers of trees as well as complementary understory and groundcover around and below. To create lasting landscapes and support a variety of organisms in the urban environment, plan a diverse, intricate, multilayered garden modeled after natural landscapes that have structural, functional, and species diversity. Such a landscape contains a wide range of site-adapted and habitat-appropriate trees, shrubs, and groundcovers, chosen based on their low resource input requirements and high ecosystem services yields.

A multilayered garden has both horizontal and vertical complexity. Varied trees of different sizes and ages, once grown, provide

An example of a multilayered landscape is Schmitz Park Preserve in West Seattle, a healthy forest remnant in the city with lush, diverse landscapes, and an abundance of wildlife.

LEFT: *Ornamental plants form a multilayered landscape.* **RIGHT:** *A multilayered shelter belt of native plants*

a canopy, with the smaller plants occupying the understory. The middle layer is usually made up of large and small shrubs; and the groundcover layer has a lively mix of perennials, biennials, grasses, and annuals, including the flowers that pollinators love.

These layers grow into an interwoven community over time. Landscapes with more plant diversity have more numerous and varied vertebrate and invertebrate populations, and they also support natural pest control processes. A wide assortment of plants will better ensure that wildlife has food and shelter throughout the year. Include a mix of both evergreen and decid-

uous species. Evergreens, particularly conifers, provide critical shelter, nesting sites, and seeds for birds and other wildlife during winter, while deciduous flowering plants provide pollen, nectar, fruit, and nuts. Birds and butterflies will appreciate all this, and their visits provide a wonderful and entertaining addition to any garden.

Shelter Belts

If you build a multilayered, complex landscape on the border of your property, it becomes a shelter belt, providing a beautiful boundary and a natural privacy belt. It is best to use dense plantings of primarily native plants for shelter belts as this helps outcompete weeds, requiring less maintenance and enhancing the area for wildlife.

Shelter belts are a natural buffer against dust pollution and noise; they also serve as windbreaks and give shade. And even though

SHELTER BELT PLANTING PLANS

Plant these shelter belts in the fall. Cluster three or more shrubs in odd numbers of the same species. While the spacing of plants always varies with the specific plant, a starting point guideline is to space your trees about 15–30 feet apart, shrubs 5–10 feet apart, and groundcovers 1–3 feet apart. The table below lists vegetation that works well in a shelter belt.

PLANT	SIZE	LANDSCAPE LAYER
PARTIAL SHADE		
Blue elderberry (*Sambucus cerulea*)	15–20 ft. tall x 8–12 ft. wide	Canopy, middle
Cascara (*Frangula purshiana*)	18–34 ft. tall x 19–17 ft. wide	Canopy
Huckleberry (*Vaccinium ovatum*)	3–10 ft. tall and wide	Middle
Red-twig dogwood (*Cornus sericea*)	10 ft. tall and wide	Middle
Salal (*Gaultheria shallon*)	2–6 ft. tall and wide	Understory
Tall Oregon grape (*Berberis aquifolium*)	5–8 ft. tall x 3–5 ft. wide	Middle
Vine maple (*Acer circinatum*)	15–25 ft. tall and wide	Canopy, middle
DRY, SUNNY SITE		
Beach strawberry (*Fragaria chiloensis*)	2–5 in. tall x 6–8 in. wide	Understory
Manzanita 'Howard McMinn' (*Arctostaphylos densiflora*)	7–10 ft. tall and wide	Middle
Mock orange (*Philadelphus lewisii*)	6–9 ft. tall x 5–7 ft. wide	Middle
Pacific serviceberry (*Amelanchier alnifolia*)	10–15 ft. tall and wide	Canopy
Prostrate ceanothus (*Ceanothus prostratus*)	3–4 in. tall x 3–7 ft. wide	Understory
Whitebeam (*Sorbus aria* 'Lutescens')	25–40 ft. tall x 20–30 ft. wide	Canopy
Yarrow (*Achillea millefolium*)	1–3 ft. tall x 1–2 ft. wide	Understory
DRY SHADE (NORTH SIDE OF HOUSE)		
Huckleberry (*Vaccinium ovatum*)	3–10 ft. tall and wide	Middle
Inside-out flower (*Vancouveria hexandra*)	1–1.5 ft. tall and wide	Understory
Salal (*Gaultheria shallon*)	2–6 ft. tall and wide	Understory
Snowberry (*Symphoricarpos albus*)	5–7 ft. tall and wide	Middle
Sword fern (*Polystichum munitum*)	3–4 ft. tall and wide	Understory
Tall Oregon grape (*Berberis aquifolium*)	5–8 ft. tall x 3–6 ft. wide	Middle
Vine maple (*Acer circinatum*)	15–25 ft. tall and wide	Canopy, middle

the mature community may protect you from prying human eyes, insects and other animals will have a full view as they find foliage, fruits, seeds, pollen, and nectar and shelter within.

All curated landscapes require ongoing monitoring and management, but once these shelter belts are established, they are likely

Waves of heaths (Erica species) grow in the border area of this Whidbey Island garden.

to be reasonably self-sufficient, resisting invasive species and requiring little maintenance and supplemental water. However, domestic pets should not be allowed in a shelter belt. Outdoor lighting can also interfere with nocturnal wildlife by disrupting their movement, biological cycles, and foraging behavior, as well as cause plants to retain their leaves in fall and delay the dormancy that prepares plants for cold weather. Therefore, do not use lights near a shelter belt, and direct all outdoor lighting downward and inward toward the home.

Plant Groupings

Another option for gardeners who appreciate a natural aesthetic is to use the same or similar plants in intermingled groupings. In my garden, waves of heaths and heathers grow in different garden areas on a southwest-facing hillside, with the shorter cultivars in the front portion of the planting beds and taller culti-

vars just behind; shrubs and trees serve as a backdrop.

If done right, such groupings can pack a visual punch, by unifying the garden and providing cohesion, as well as creating stronger edges to the landscape. The objective is to design and create plant communities that match local site conditions, while also

When designing your plantings, leave stumps, snags, logs, and disease-free leaves where they lie.

LEFT: *Keep in mind that as new plants grow and compete with one another and with those already established for nutrients, light, and space, the dynamics of the community will change. So plan ahead and situate them based on their individual needs.* **RIGHT:** *The plant in the center has had its roots properly loosened after being removed from its container.*

considering their balance, relative size, scale, and proportion. Functionally, the new plants should be similar to the natives, able to carry out similar dynamic ecological processes and be mostly self-sufficient once established.

INSTALLING PLANTS

Once you have decided on plants that are suited to your specific site and lifestyle, you need to select the specific specimens from those available at the nursery. Buy well-grown, healthy, and vigorous plants from a reputable nursery that will stand behind their merchandise.

Perform a visual checkup on each plant before you purchase it. Lay containerized plants on their sides and gently remove them from the containers to inspect roots. Plants with normal, well-developed branches and a vigorous root system will establish and grow

the best. Avoid woody plants with circling or kinked roots, or with branches that form narrow angles with the trunk. Stay away from root-bound plants or those in containers where the root crown or flare is not clearly visible.

In general, small plants transplant more successfully than larger plants, experience less transplant shock, adapt more quickly to the site, require less irrigation to establish, and are less expensive. Plugs or 4-inch pots are suitable for grasses and herbaceous plants. Plants fare best if installed during periods when they get adequate moisture and temperatures are not too cold. These conditions help enable the plants to recover from transplant shock, develop good root systems, and prepare to make new top growth. For example, in the western Pacific Northwest, where the summers are dry and winters are relatively warm and wet, it is best to plant in the fall.

Woody Shrubs

Woody shrubs are generally purchased in containers and are transplanted bare root; follow the procedure for trees described in Chapter 4, Trees. Move the plant using the container rather than the plant's trunk or branches. Be sure to inspect the roots and buy only those plants that appear free of root defects.

Herbaceous Perennials

Handle and transplant herbaceous perennials and seedlings gently, as some perennials, such as heaths and heathers, do not like their roots pulled apart before they are planted. During the planting process keep the plant roots moist at all times. I always do my planting early in the morning on cool, cloudy days to minimize the likelihood of the roots drying out.

It's best to plant bare root herbaceous perennials in the fall, to allow the roots to get established during the winter and spring months before the dry summer. Planting in the spring when the soil is moist is also fine for bare root perennials. Container-grown perennials can be planted any time of the year as long as the ground is not frozen or soaking wet. However, it is important to keep the plants moist after planting.

How to Plant Them

Planting perennials is relatively easy. Success depends on good soil preparation, proper planting, and keeping plants well watered. Planting container-grown perennials is sim-

TOP: *Gently set the root ball of a container-grown plant on a firm mound in the center of the planting hole and spread the roots radially and horizontally.* **BOTTOM:** *Make sure the trunk flare on top of the root mass is slightly above the surrounding grade.*

ilar to the process for bare root, but requires a few extra steps.

Bare Root Perennials

1. Loosen the soil with a spading fork and remove all the weeds.
2. Use your garden trowel to make a hole just deep and wide enough to set in the clump such that all the roots are buried while leaving the stems and shoots aboveground.

After filling in around the roots with native soil from the planting hole, give the plant a thorough watering.

3. Using your hand, backfill with native soil and firm the soil around the stem.
4. Water well.

Container-Grown Perennials

1. Loosen the soil with a spading fork and remove all the weeds.
2. Set the plant on its side and gently tap it out of the container rather than pulling it out by its stem.
3. If you see circling roots, gently tease them apart by pulling on them.
4. Prepare the hole and set in the root ball as for bare root perennials.
5. Fill in with native soil from the hole and firm it around the stem.
6. Water well to remove the air spaces and settle the soil.

You'll be able to tell if you've made a good match between site conditions and the needs of the plant by the plant's health, and its ability to maintain desirable characteristics while requiring little water, fertilizer, soil amendments, or pesticides. Native animals will use it for food, shelter, or nesting sites. It should grow steadily but not aggressively, without calling for you to constantly prune, deadhead, shear, or mow.

SHRUBS AND PERENNIALS FOR EACH SEASON

The following plant list, organized by the predominant season in which each plant flowers, includes predominantly drought-tolerant plants that grow well in the Pacific Northwest and are particularly attractive to pollinators. I've tested these in my own garden. Each entry lists the plant's mature size, light requirements, soil preferences, USDA zone (see map in Chapter 2), and Sunset zone (see Resources) as well as whether it is drought tolerant.

Native Ornamentals

Natives are not only great for attracting pollinators and other wildlife, but they can add an element of local character and place to Pacific Northwest yards. There are many to choose from, but the following are some of the best, in my opinion. For the benefits of planting natives in your yard, see Native Species in Chapter 4.

Fall

DOUGLAS ASTER

Symphotrichum subspicatum
Perennial

Douglas aster, Symphyotrichum subspicatum

A rhizomatous perennial wildflower, Douglas aster has branched stems and light blue to purple, asterlike flowers.

Mature size: 2–3 ft. tall and wide
Light requirement: Full sun to partial shade
Soil: Moist, well draining
Pollinators: Butterflies
USDA zone: 6–9
Sunset zone: Not available
Other: Can be weedy.

Winter

WESTERN BEAKED HAZELNUT

Corylus cornuta var. californica
Tree/shrub

This graceful, small arching tree/shrub, often multistemmed, provides long, dangling creamy-white male catkins in winter, whose pollen drifts to pollinate the tiny bright red flowers clinging to the stems. The flowers later develop into edible hazelnuts in beaked husks.

Mature size: 5–12 ft. tall and wide
Light requirement: Full sun to partial shade

Soil: Moist, well draining
Pollinators: Wind
USDA zone: 4–8
Sunset zone: 2–9, 14–20
Other: Drought tolerant; birds and mammals eat the nuts; provides good cover and nesting sites for birds.

Spring

COLUMBINE

Aquilegia sp. and hybrids
Perennial

This woodland plant has lacy foliage, delicate nodding flowers with nectar-bearing spurs, and color-contrasting sepals and petals.

Mature size: 1–3 ft. tall x 0.5–2 ft. wide
Light requirement: Full sun to partial shade
Soil: Moist, well draining
Pollinators: Bees (bumble, native) hummingbirds, butterflies
USDA zone: 3–9
Sunset zone : Varies by species

Western columbine, Aquilegia formosa

CURRANT

Ribes sp.
Deciduous shrub

Native to the western coast mountain ranges from California to British Columbia, the red flowering currant (*Ribes sanguineum*) has drooping clusters of pink to red flowers that begin to bloom in March. The cultivars 'White Icicle' currant and 'Album' have white flowers.

Mature size: 8–10 ft. tall x 3–12 ft. wide

Light requirement: Full sun to partial shade

Soil: Moist, well draining

Pollinators: Butterflies, hummingbirds

USDA zone: Varies by species; *R. sanguineum*, 5–8

Sunset zone: Varies by species; *R. sanguineum*, A3, 4–9, 14–24

Other: Drought tolerant

ELDERBERRY, BLUE AND RED

Sambucus caerulea and *Sambucus racemosa*
Deciduous shrub

The blue elderberry (*Sambucus caerulea*), native to the west coast of the United States, has flat-topped clusters of white flowers in spring and summer. The blue to blue-black berries are attractive to birds and excellent for making jellies, jams, and pies, but should not be eaten raw. In contrast, the red elderberry (*Sambucus racemosa*) has white flowers in dome-shaped clusters, followed by bright red inedible berries.

Mature size: 8–30 ft. tall x 8–20 ft. wide

Light requirement: Full sun to partial shade

Soil: Moist, well draining

Pollinators: Hummingbirds, butterflies

USDA zone: Blue elderberry, 4–8; red elderberry, 5–8

Sunset zone: Blue elderberry, 2–24, H1; red elderberry, A2–A3, 1–6

Other: Blue elderberry is drought tolerant.

EVERGREEN HUCKLEBERRY

Vaccinium ovatum
Evergreen shrub

This ornamental shrub has bell-shaped flowers in spring, followed by colorful edible berries attractive to birds and humans. It is native to the Pacific Coast with springtime bronzy-reddish leaves that turn a lustrous green. It has white-and-pinkish flowers and shiny black berries.

Mature size: 3–10 ft. tall and wide

Light requirement: Full sun to full shade

Soil: Organic-rich, acidic, moist, well draining

Pollinators: Bees, butterflies, hummingbirds

USDA zone: 7–9

Sunset zone: 4–7, 14–17, 22–24

Other: Drought tolerant, deer resistant

LUPINE

Lupinus sp.
Annual/perennial/shrub

Lupine's flowers grow in dense spikes at the end of the stem. Many wonderful hybrids have been developed from plants native to the West Coast. These hybrids are stur-

Blue elderberry, Sambucus caerulea

Burk's lupine, Lupinus polyphyllus *var.* burkei

dier than the original species as they do not require staking, and they are long-lived and have a long bloom period if the flowers are deadheaded.

Mature size: 1–6 ft. tall x 1–8 ft. wide
Light requirement: Full sun to partial shade
Soil: Moist to dry, well draining
Pollinators: Bees (bumble, mason), hummingbirds; host plant for butterflies.
USDA and Sunset zones: Varies by species

OCEANSPRAY

Holodiscus discolor
Deciduous shrub

This shrub native to the West Coast mountain ranges has plumes of creamy-white flowers in late spring/early summer, which age to tannish gold.

Mature size: 8–16 ft. tall x 4–15 ft. wide
Light requirement: Partial sun to partial shade
Soil: Moist to dry, gravelly, well draining
Pollinators: Bees, wasps, syrphid flies; host plant for butterflies.
USDA zone: 5–9
Sunset zone: 1–9, 14–19
Other: Drought tolerant

TALL OREGON GRAPE

Berberis [Mahonia] aquifolium
Evergreen shrub

Native to the West Coast and primarily west of the Cascades, this shrub has spikelike clusters of yellow flowers in late winter/early spring followed by blue edible berries. It typically has prickly, glossy green leaves, each composed of five to nine leaflets. New leaves may emerge bronze, and some of the mature leaves may become red or purple, particularly in cold winters.

Mature size: 5–8 ft. tall x 3–5 ft. wide
Light requirement: Full sun to full shade, partial shade to full shade in hottest climates
Soil: Moist to dry, well draining
Pollinators: Bees (bumble, mason), butterflies
USDA zone: 5–8
Sunset zone: 2–12, 14–24
Other: Drought tolerant, deer resistant

Tall Oregon grape, Berberis aquifolium

Blue mountain beardtongue, Penstemon pennellianus

Summary

These daisylike flowers have two or more flower rays surrounding a usually yellow disk. I primarily grow the Pacific Northwest native *Erigeron speciosus* for its soft violet flowers.

Mature size: 1–2 ft. tall x 1.5–3 ft. wide

Light requirement: Full sun to partial shade

Soil: Moist to dry, well draining

Pollinators: Bees, butterflies, moths

USDA zone: Varies by species; *E. speciosus*, 2–8

Sunset zone: Varies by species; *E. speciosus*, 1–9, 14–24

Other: Drought tolerant

STONECROP

Sedum sp.
Perennial

These tough, low-maintenance herbaceous plants have thick stems, fleshy leaves, and clusters of small, star-shaped flowers. One of the best is the Pacific Northwest native *Sedum spathulifolium*.

Mature size: 0.3–5 ft. tall x 1–5 ft. wide

Light requirment: Full sun to partial shade

Soil: Well draining

Pollinators: Bees (bumble, carpenter), butterflies

USDA and Sunset zones: Varies by species

Other: Drought tolerant

YARROW

Achillea millefolium
Perennial

Sweet, fernlike leaves and colorful, flat-topped flower clusters grace this herbaceous perennial native to much of North America, including the Pacific Northwest.

Mature size: 1–3 ft. tall x 1–2 ft. wide

Light requirement: Full sun

Soil: Well draining

Pollinators: Bees, butterflies, moths

Summer

BEARDTONGUE

Penstemon sp.
Perennial

This Pacific Northwest native has dense spikes of colorful tubular flowers. Provide the plants with plenty of room, as they don't like to be crowded.

Mature size: 1–3 ft. tall and wide

Light requirement: Full sun to partial shade, partial shade in hottest climates

Soil: Well draining, tolerant of poor soils

Pollinators: Bees (bumble, leafcutter, sweat), moths, butterflies, hummingbirds

USDA zone: 4–9

Sunset zone: Varies by species

Other: Drought and heat tolerant

FLEABANE

Erigeron sp.
Annual-biennial-perennial

LEFT: *Yarrow*, Achillea millefolium RIGHT: *Fall-blooming asters*, Symphyotrichum *species*

USDA zone: 3–9

Sunset zone: A1–A3; 1–24

Other: Drought tolerant, has a tendency to spread.

Nonnative Ornamentals

Plant nonnatives from each of the following sections to add beauty and interest to your garden in all four seasons. For the benefits of planting nonnatives in your yard, see Nonnative Species in Chapter 4.

Fall

ASTERS

Symphyotrichum sp. and hybrids
Perennial

> Asters are daisylike herbaceous perennials with starry-shaped flower heads.

Mature size: 0.5–6 ft. tall x 0.5–2 ft. wide

Light requirement: Full sun to partial shade

Soil: Moist, well draining

Pollinators: Butterflies

USDA zone: 4–8

Sunset zone: Varies by species, most species 1–24

Other: Drought tolerant; divide every 2–3 years.

BLUE MIST SHRUB

Caryopteris x *clandonensis*
Shrub

> **This hybrid of Asian natives has attractive blue flowers from midsummer to frost.**

Mature size: 3–4 ft. tall and wide

Light requirement: Full sun to partial shade

Soil: Well draining

Pollinators: Bees, butterflies, hummingbirds

USDA zone: 5–9

Sunset zone: 2b–9, 14–24

Other: Drought tolerant

CRAPE MYRTLE

Lagerstroemia sp.
Deciduous shrub/tree

> This plant with four-season interest has showy flowers, attractive bark, and bright fall color. In regions with cool summers, select cold-hardy, mildew-resistant varieties.

LEFT: *Rosemary*, Rosmarinus officinalis *'Irene'* RIGHT: *Sage*, Salvia *species*

Mature size: 2–20+ ft. tall x 2–15 ft. wide

Light requirement: Full sun

Soil: Well draining

Pollinators: Bees, wasps, syrphid flies

USDA zone: 7–9

Sunset zone: 7–10, 12–14, 18–21

Other: Drought tolerant, deer resistant

HEATHS AND HEATHERS

Erica vagans and *Calluna vulgaris*
Evergreen shrub

> Excellent evergreen groundcovers, these plants have attractive foliage and a large variety of colorful flowers blooming late summer into fall.

Mature size: 0.5–3 ft. tall x 0.5–6 ft. wide

Light requirement: Full sun to partial sun

Soil: Well draining

Pollinators: Bees

USDA zone: 5–8 for both

Sunset zone: *E. vagans*, 1a, 2–6, 15–17; *C. vulgaris*, 3b–6, 16–17, 20–24

Other: Drought tolerant, deer resistant, both also bloom in summer.

ROSEMARY 'IRENE'

Rosmarinus officinalis 'Irene'
Shrub

> This cold-hardy prostrate cultivar spreads 3–6 feet or more, and its deep blue flowers bloom in spring and fall.

Mature size: 1.5 ft. tall x 6+ ft. wide (spreading)

Light requirement: Full sun

Soil: Well draining

Pollinators: Bees, butterflies, moths

USDA zone: 7–10

Sunset zone: 4–24

Other: Drought tolerant, deer resistant, also blooms in spring.

SAGE

Fall-blooming *Salvia* sp. and hybrids
Perennial/shrub

> Salvia belongs to the mint family. It has square stems. The long-blooming flowers blossom from terminal spikes, usually consisting of colorful tubes with two lips differing in length. Hundreds of varieties, including summer bloomers, are available.

Mature size: Varies by species

Light requirement: Full sun

Soil: Well draining

Pollinators: Bees (bumble, digger, large carpenter, leaf-cutter, mason), butterflies, hummingbirds

USDA and Sunset zones: Varies by species

Other: Some drought tolerant

SHOWY STONECROP

Hylotelephium spectabile
Perennial

> These tall herbaceous plants have thick stems, fleshy leaves, and tight flower heads.

Mature size: 18–24 in. tall x 12–24 in. wide

Light requirement: Full sun to partial shade

Soil: Well draining

Pollinators: Bees, butterflies, hummingbirds

USDA zone: 4–9

Sunset zone: A1–A3; 1–10, 14–24

Other: Tolerant of drought and seasonal wetness

SUNFLOWER

Helianthus annuus
Annual

> These big daisylike flowers are native to the central United States and have bright yellow petals with brown or maroon disklike centers. Their seeds are attractive to birds. New varieties may have red, orange, or white blooms.

Mature size: 3–15 ft. tall x 0.5–2 ft. wide

Light requirement: Full sun

Soil: Well draining, slightly acidic to somewhat alkaline, loamy or sandy

Pollinators: Bees (bumble, leafcutter, longhorn, sweat), wasps, beetles, butterflies, flies

USDA and Sunset zones: Not applicable to annuals

Other: Drought tolerant; avoid pollen-less or double-petal varieties, plant after last frost in spring.

White Snakeroot, Ageratina altissima

WHITE SNAKEROOT

Ageratina altissima (*Eupatorium rugosum* 'Chocolate')
Perennial

> This native of the east coast of the United States has deep-brown stems and leaves, and fluffy white flowers in late summer and fall.

Mature size: 3–4 ft. tall x 2 ft. wide

Light requirement: Partial shade to full sun

Soil: Moist, well-draining, alkaline

Pollinators: Bees, butterflies

USDA zone: 4–8

Sunset zone: 1–10, 14–17

Other: Poisonous for animals and humans

Winter

HEATHS

Erica x *darleyensis* and *Erica carnea*
Evergreen shrub

> Heaths are excellent long-blooming ground-covers. Many have bronze foliage in winter and cream-colored new growth. Shear off old flowers annually to create bushier plants.

Hellebores, Helleborus species

Mature size: 0.5–1.5 ft. tall x 0.5–5 ft. wide
Light requirement: Full sun to partial shade
Soil: Well draining
Pollinators: Bees
USDA zone: 6–8
Sunset zone: 2–10, 14–24
Other: Drought tolerant, deer resistant

HELLEBORES

Helleborus sp. and hybrids
Perennial

> These long-lived plants have pretty, cup-shaped flowers and leathery foliage.

Mature size: 1–3 ft. tall and wide
Light requirement: Full shade to partial shade
Soil: Well draining
Pollinators: Bumblebees, bees, flies; all types of insects can pollinate the flowers effectively.
USDA zone: 5–8
Sunset zone: Varies by species
Other: Divide every 3–6 years; deer resistant, drought and frost tolerant.

MAHONIA HYBRIDS

Berberis x *media*
Evergreen shrub

> These Asian hybrids are tough, adaptable plants with striking foliage and huge sprays of bright yellow, nectar-rich flowers, followed by blue to black fruit that birds love.

Mature size: 5–15 ft. tall x 6–12 ft. wide
Light requirement: Full sun to partial shade
Soil: Well draining
Pollinators: Bees
USDA zone: 7–9
Sunset zone: 6–9, 14–24
Other: Drought tolerant

SWEETBOX

Sarcococca sp.
Evergreen shrub

> These shrubs have glossy, dark green foliage and fragrant white flowers followed by shiny red or black berries.

Mahonia hybrids, Berberis (*Mahonia*) x media

Viburnum, Viburnum bodnantense 'Charles Lamont'

Mature size: 1.5–6 ft. tall x 3–8 ft. wide
Light requirement: Full shade to partial shade
Soil: Rich in organic matter, well draining
Pollinators: Bees
USDA zone: 6–8; except *S. ruscifolia*, 7–8
Sunset zone: 4–9, 14–24

VIBURNUM

Viburnum x *bodnantense* and *Viburnum tinus*
Deciduous shrub

> *Viburnum* x *bodnantense* has crusty bark and pink buds that become fragrant pinkish flowers as early as December. The small berries and green leaves come in spring and turn into shades of scarlet in fall. *V. tinus* is an evergreen shrub with dark green foliage, fragrant white to light pink flowers in winter, followed by metallic blue-black fruit.

Mature size: 6–12 ft. tall x 3–6 ft. wide
Light requirement: Full sun to partial shade
Soil: Well draining
Pollinators: Bees, butterflies
USDA zone: *V. bodnantense*, 5–9; *V. tinus*, 8–10
Sunset zone: *V. bodnantense*, 4–9, 14–24; *V. tinus*, 4–10

WINTER FLOWERING HONEYSUCKLE

Lonicera x *purpusii* 'Winter Beauty'
Deciduous shrub

> This is a strong, fast-growing shrub with green leaves. The small, sweetly fragrant white flowers with yellow stamens top brown young stems.

Mature size: 5–8 ft. tall and wide
Light requirement: Full sun to partial shade
Soil: Moist, well draining
Pollinators: Butterflies, hummingbirds
USDA zone: 5–9
Sunset zone: Not available
Other: Drought tolerant

Spring

CANDYTUFT

Iberis sempervirens
Perennial

> The most common candytuft, native to southern and western Europe, is the evergreen *Iberis sempervirens*. It has dark green leaves and an abundance of pure white flower clusters. In mild climates it begins to bloom in late winter.

Candytuft, Iberis sempervirens

LEFT: *Manzanita,* Arctostaphylos *species* RIGHT: *Bee balm,* Monarda didyma

Mature size: 12–18 in. tall and wide

Light requirement: Full sun to partial shade

Soil: Well draining

Pollinators: Bees, butterflies, moths

USDA zone: 3–9

Sunset zone: 1–24

Other: Drought tolerant, deer resistant

MANZANITA

Arctostaphylos sp.
Evergreen shrub

This shrub, with its reddish to purple bark and intricate branch pattern, is native to the West, primarily California. It has small urn-shaped white or pinkish flowers and red to brown berrylike fruit attractive to birds. A great manzanita for the Pacific Northwest is the 7- to 10-foot *A. densiflora* 'Howard McMinn'.

Mature size: 1–10 ft. tall and wide

Light requirement: Full sun to partial sun

Soil: Dry, well draining

Pollinators: Hummingbirds, moths, butterflies

USDA zone: Varies by species; *A. densiflora,* 8–10

Sunset zone: Varies by species; *A. densiflora,* 7–9, 14–21

Other: Drought tolerant

Summer

BEE BALM

Monarda didyma
Perennial

This member of the mint family is native to eastern North America and features tubular two-lipped bright red flowers. To minimize problems with powdery mildew, provide good air circulation by planting it in an open position and not crowding it with other plants.

Mature size: 2–4 ft. tall x 2–3 ft. wide

Light requirement: Full sun to partial shade

Soil: Moist, well draining

Pollinators: Bees, hummingbirds, butterflies

USDA zone: 4–9

Sunset zone: A2–A3; 1–11, 14–17

Other: Divide every 3–4 years.

BLAZING STAR

Liatris spicata
Perennial

This prairie native from eastern and central North America has narrow, grassy-looking leaves and bears tall fuzzy spikes of bright purple or magenta flowers.

Mature size: 2–4 ft. tall x 1–2 ft. wide

Light requirement: Full sun to partial sun

Soil: Well draining

Pollinators: Bees, butterflies

USDA zone: 3–9

Sunset zone: A2–A3; 1–10, 14–24

Other: Drought tolerant; divide every 3–4 years.

CATMINT

Nepata x *faassenii*
Perennial

Easy to grow, hardy, and long-lived, catmint bears loose spikes of fragrant lavender-blue flowers above its equally fragrant gray-green leaves. To promote continued bloom, cut faded flower stems.

Mature size: 1–3 ft. tall and wide

Light requirement: Full sun to partial shade

Soil: Well draining

Pollinators: Bees (bumble, carder, digger, honey, mason), butterflies, moths

USDA zone: Varies by species

Sunset zone: Most 1–24

Other: Drought tolerant, deer resistant

HYSSOP

Agastache sp. and hybrids
Perennial

This plant, primarily native to North America, bears upright spikes of two-lipped flowers.

Mature size: 2–5 ft. tall x 1.5–2 ft. wide

Light requirement: Full sun to partial shade

Soil: Well draining

Pollinators: Bees, butterflies, hummingbirds

USDA and Sunset zones: Varies by species

Other: Drought tolerant, deer and rabbit resistant

LAVENDER

Lavandula sp.
Perennial

Native to the Mediterranean region, this shrub is famous for its fragrant flowers and foliage. Leaves are typically gray green or sil-

Lavender, Lavandula angustifolia, is a great source of nectar for many kinds of bees.

LEFT: *Italian oregano*, Origanum vulgare RIGHT: *Russian sage*, Perovskia atriplicifolia

very green and the flowers are blue, purple, or white.

Mature size: 0.7–4 ft. tall x 2–5 ft. wide

Light requirement: Full sun

Soil: Well draining

Pollinators: Bees (bumble, digger, large carpenter, leaf-cutter), butterflies, moths

USDA and Sunset zones: Varies by species

Other: Drought tolerant

OREGANO

Origanum sp.
Perennial

This herb is a member of the mint family and has tight clusters of small flowers with colorful bracts and aromatic foliage.

Mature size: 0.4–2.5 ft. tall x 1–3 ft. wide

Light requirement: Full sun

Soil: Well draining

Pollinators: Bees, butterflies

USDA zone: Most species 5–9

Sunset zone: Varies by species

Other: Drought tolerant

RUSSIAN SAGE

Perovskia atriplicifolia
Perennial

This airy-looking plant is native to Afghanistan, Pakistan, Iran, and Tibet. It has tall stems clothed in gray-green leaves, topped with sprays of lavender-blue flowers.

Mature size: 3–4 ft. tall and wide

Light requirement: Full sun

Soil: Well draining

Pollinators: Bees (carpenter, honey, leafcutter), butterflies, flies

USDA zone: 4–9

Sunset zone: 2–24

Other: Drought and heat tolerant; cut nearly to the ground in spring.

THYME

Thymus sp.
Perennial

This Mediterranean native and member of the mint family has small, fragrant leaves that are topped with great numbers of small flowers. The mat-forming or prostrate types make good groundcovers.

Mature size: 0.1–1.5 ft. tall x 1–3 ft. wide

Light requirement: Full sun to partial sun

Soil: Well draining

Pollinators: Bees (bumble, digger, mason, sweat, yellow-faced)

USDA zone: 4–9

Sunset zone: Most species 1–24

Other: Attracts beneficial insects.

PERENNIALS FOR EATING

Harvesting food from your garden is a great and effective way to minimize your use of resources and impact on the environment. The majority of the food in urban areas comes from large commercial farms growing annual crops that require regular tillage of the soil and usually extensive use of irrigation, chemical fertilizers, and pesticides. Unfortunately, repeated tilling increases the rate of decomposition of soil organic matter, degrades soil structure, kills earthworms, and destroys soil fungal networks. It also increases nutrient runoff and erosion and is not sustainable over time.

Perennial crops do not require regular tillage and can readily be grown using organic methods, with minimal use of chemical fertilizers and pesticides and less fresh water for irrigation. Also, perennial crops generally demand fewer natural resources and less maintenance than annual crops. Once established, perennial edible plants need relatively little care while providing many years of harvest. These perennials help build healthy soil by improving porosity, water-holding capacity, and structure. They can provide habitat for beneficial organisms and help extend the harvest season. Many perennial edible plants can be readily integrated with ornamental landscape plants and be attractive as well.

Native Edibles

Northwest natives can provide food and habitat not only for wildlife, but also for your family. The Northwest native plant palette has many plants that provide us with tasty and nutritious berries, roots (such as the bulbs of the giant camas and the common camas, which Native Americans ate raw in the past), and leaves (such as oxalis).

EVERGREEN HUCKLEBERRY

Vaccinium ovatum
Evergreen shrub

This small black berry ripens in the fall and can be eaten fresh or used to make jams and preserves.

Mature size: 3–10 ft. tall and wide

Light requirement: Full sun to full shade

Soil: Organic-rich, acidic, moist, well draining

Pollinators: Bees, butterflies, hummingbirds

USDA zone: 7–9

Sunset zone: 4–7, 14–17, 22–24

Other: Drought tolerant, deer resistant

GOLDEN CURRANT

Ribes aureum
Perennial

This ripe, pectin-rich, flavorful berry is golden yellow to dark red.

Mature size: 4–6 ft. tall and wide
Light requirement: Full sun to partial shade
Soil: Moist, well draining
Pollinators: Bees, butterflies, hummingbirds
USDA zone: 3–8
Sunset zone: A2–A3; 1–12, 14–23
Other: Drought tolerant, highly adaptable

GOOSEBERRY

Ribes divaricatum var. *divaricatum*
Perennial

This sweet-tasting berry is black when ripe.

Mature size: 4–8 ft. tall and wide
Light requirement: Full sun to partial shade
Soil: Moist, well draining
Pollinators: Bees (bumble, andrenid, honey)
USDA zone: 7–9
Sunset zone: Not available
Other: Highly adaptable

SALAL

Gaultheria shallon
Evergreen shrub

The dark blue, mealy berry can be eaten fresh but more often is mixed with other berries to make jam, preserves, or pie.

Mature size: 2–6 ft. tall and wide
Light requirement: Partial sun to full shade
Soil: Moist, well draining
Pollinators: Bees, butterflies, hummingbirds
USDA zone: 6–9
Sunset zone: 4–7, 14–17

Strawberry, Fragaria chiloensis

Other: Adaptable, tolerant of poor soils, deer resistant, drought tolerant

SALMONBERRY

Rubus spectabilis
Perennial

Mildly sweet when mature, this berry is yellow red.

Mature size: 2–6 ft. tall and wide
Light requirement: Full sun to full shade
Soil: Moist
Pollinators: Bumblebees, hummingbirds
USDA zone: 5–9
Sunset zone: Not available
Other: Adaptable

STRAWBERRY

Fragaria chiloensis
Perennial

These edible berries are red when ripe.

Mature size: 4–8 in. tall and wide
Light requirement: Full sun to partial sun, afternoon shade in hottest climate
Soil: Sandy, well draining
Pollinators: Bees, butterflies, syrphid flies

USDA zone: 5–9

Sunset zone: 4–24, H1

Other: Cut back growth annually in early spring.

WHITE BARK RASPBERRY

Rubus leucodermis
Perennial

> This ripe berry high in anthocyanin is dark purple to nearly black. It differs from the commercial-variety raspberries we buy in the store as these are derived from the red raspberry *Rubus idaeus* or the black raspberry *Rubus occidentalis* or their hybrids.

Mature size: 8 ft. tall x 3 ft. wide

Light requirement: Full sun to full shade

Soil: Well draining

Pollinators: Bees, butterflies

USDA zone: 5–9

Sunset zone: Not available

Nonnative Edibles

In general in the Northwest, perennial vegetables do best in full sun and need good garden loam. The following is a list of perennial vegetables that are great additions to Northwest gardens.

- *Asparagus*: Although asparagus takes a number of years to get established and yield a reasonable harvest, you will know the wait was well worth it when you cook and eat the delicious freshly picked stalks.
- *Chicory*: The chicory plant is attractive with its bright blue "bachelor's buttons" flowers. The somewhat bitter leaves are used raw in salads or can boiled first to reduce their bitterness.

Give rhubarb plenty of space to grow.

- *Lincolnshire spinach*: The leaves and shoots can be steamed and eaten. The flower buds taste similar to broccoli.
- *Lovage*: Similar to celery; the raw leaves are used in salads and the roots are eaten cooked.
- *Miner's lettuce or winter purslane*: A tasty salad green native to California, this tastes similar to spinach when cooked.

Always plant more than one cultivar of blueberry.

- *Rhubarb*: The rather tart, red stalks of rhubarb are great when paired with sweet fruit, such as strawberries, for making jams, preserves, or pies.
- *Sorrel*: Harvested in early spring, this lemony-flavored vegetable is used in cooking sauces and soups, but it also can be eaten raw.
- *Wild arugula*: This green has a sharper bite than store-bought arugula and is a nice addition to salads and egg dishes.

Nonnative Edible Berries

Many varieties of berry crops grow well in the Pacific Northwest, provided they are planted on an appropriate site and given proper soil conditions—full sun, well-drained soil rich in organic matter—and care. Blueberries can produce fruit for 40 years or more, blackberries and red raspberries can be productive for 15 to 20 years, while strawberries provide fruit for up to 5 years. Other types of fruit not detailed here that can be grown in the Pacific Northwest include lingonberry, highbush cranberries, chokeberry, and kiwifruit.

Blackberry

There are three types of cultivated blackberries: trailing, semierect, and erect. Trailing and semierect blackberries require a trellis for support; however, it is advisable to trellis all three types of blackberries. Blackberries need soil with a pH between 5.5 and 7. Prune a few inches off new canes of erect blackberries when they get about 3–4 feet tall to encourage lateral branching.

Be aware that erect blackberries sucker from their roots, so if you want to avoid having a hedgerow of blackberries, then plant the semierect or trailing varieties. Prune the semierect canes once they grow to 4–5 feet tall to produce lateral branching. For trailing blackberries, train the canes to grow on a multiple-wire trellis. By the second year these canes will bear fruit. Keep the new canes growing away from the older fruit-bearing canes by training them along the ground beneath the bearing canes. Once the bearing canes die and are removed, the new canes can be trained on the trellis.

Highbush Blueberry

Highbush blueberries have attractive white or pink blossoms in spring and colorful leaves in autumn. Plant in soil with a pH between 4.5 and 5.5. It is important to plant more than one cultivar to ensure good pollination; also, select cultivars that ripen at different times to ensure the fruit will be available for a longer period. Blueberries have shallow, fibrous roots, so water them regularly (preferably by drip irrigation) during dry periods.

To prevent birds from stripping all the ripening blueberries from your plants, you can drape bird netting over the bushes just as the berries begin to turn blue, but it's easy for birds to get caught in the netting and they may even die as a result. Although there is no perfect remedy, you can try chemical repellents or auditory scare devices, though they are usually effective only in the short term. The alternative I like best is to provide a different food source for the birds. It can be choice bird food in feeders near your blueberries, or an alternate berry crop that the birds prefer planted near your blueberries. With a little luck you may be able to sit back, enjoy watching the birds, *and* still have a good crop of blueberries.

Black or Red Currant

Like gooseberries, currants are hosts for white pine blister rust and vulnerable to powdery mildew, so select cultivars that are resistant to both. Most red currants do not require more than one cultivar for fruit production. However, if you plant more than one cultivar to provide cross-pollination, you will get larger fruit. For some black currant cultivars a second cultivar may be required for pollination and fruit production. Plant in soil with a pH between 6 and 6.5; space red currants 3–4 feet apart and black currants 8–10 feet apart to permit good air circulation. Prune in late winter to improve air circulation, or remove damaged and diseased canes and canes older than 3 years. Try to retain an equal proportion of 1-, 2-, and 3-year-old canes, as these plants fruit primarily on 2- and 3-year-old wood. Black currants are most productive on 1-year-old wood. Therefore, prune to retain strong 1-year-old shoots and some 2- or 3-year-old shoots with a lot of 1-year-old growth. As currants ripen over a 2-week period, you should be able to harvest nearly all the berries in two pickings. For black currants, pick individual berries; for red currants pick the whole clusters and

Summer-bearing raspberries provide the best fruit.

winter to improve air circulation or to remove damaged and diseased canes and canes older than 3 years. Try to retain an equal proportion of 1-, 2-, and 3-year-old canes, as these plants fruit primarily on 2- and 3-year-old wood. Gooseberries ripen over a 4–6 week period; pick them individually when ripe.

Red Raspberry

Plant red raspberries in soil with a pH between 6 and 7. For a high volume of the best freezing quality, plant summer-bearing raspberry, which ripens in June/July. The canes of this perennial plant are biennial, so it takes them 2 years to bear fruit. Pick the fruit every few days when the berries are dry and refrigerate them as soon as possible. Remove the fruit-bearing canes that die after they bear fruit. To maintain vigor, apply a slow-release organic fertilizer in early spring.

remove the berries from the stem just before processing.

Gooseberry

Gooseberries are hosts for white pine blister rust—which can do considerable damage to susceptible five-needle pines—and vulnerable to powdery mildew, so select cultivars that are resistant to both. Most gooseberries do not require more than one cultivar for fruit production. However, if you plant more than one cultivar to provide cross-pollination, you will get larger fruit. Plant 3–4 feet apart in soil with a pH between 6 and 6.5. Prune in late

Strawberry

Strawberries prefer soil with a pH between 5.8 and 6.5. The first step is deciding which type of strawberry to plant: day-neutral, ever-bearing, or June-bearing. For homeowners who just want fresh strawberries for their families, day-neutrals are a good choice because you can harvest quality fresh fruit with good flavor nearly continuously throughout most of the growing season. Unlike day-neutrals, ever-bearers produce two crops, one in June and another in the fall. June-bearers produce fruit in June/July. The flavor and size of the berry will vary with the cultivar.

The most common training methods for strawberries are the *hill system* and the *matted row system*. For ever-bearers and day-neutrals that do not put out a lot of runners, use the hill system. Set plants 12–15 inches apart in double- or triple-wide rows with about 2 feet between the groupings; remove runners that creep between the rows throughout the growing season. For the matted row system, which you should use for June-bearing plants, set plants about 15 inches apart in the row with 3–4 feet between rows. Allow the runners from the "mother" plants to take root and form a matted row about 18 inches wide, while keeping about 2 feet clear between rows. The matted row system is often used for June-bearing plants because they put out a lot of runners.

Remove all the flowers from June-bearing plants during the first year to enhance leaf and crown growth. In contrast, for day-neutrals and ever-bearers remove only the first flush of flowers formed before July and then let the flowers and fruit develop thereafter. Remove all runners that have not rooted by the end of August. Use mulch between plants to suppress weeds and conserve moisture. As strawberries have shallow roots, irrigation is necessary during dry periods. Pick all fruit when ripe, as overripe fruit left on the plant will make pest and disease problems more likely. It is best to wash the fruit just before using it.

ANNUAL EDIBLES

Growing annual edible crops requires considerably more effort and planning than growing perennial edible crops, but a small, intensely planted area managed with organic methods can yield lots of fresh vegetables for your family. Eating vegetables from right outside your door will reduce the carbon emissions from the transport and refrigeration storage of food, and organic practices help reduce the amount of fertilizers and pesticides being washed into our waterways. The tips below center on using raised beds or containers, which are ideal for home gardeners in the cooler portions of the Northwest because they help the soil warm up faster and extend the relatively short growing season, but these tips can also be applied to beds planted directly

A cold frame can extend the vegetable growing season.

LEFT: *Carrots freshly pulled from the garden* **RIGHT:** *Raised beds are ideal for growing herbs and vegetables.*

in the ground, which are better in areas with warmer summers.

- In a cool, maritime climate it is essential to pick a sunny, warm location for your vegetable bed and to use a garden mix soil rich in organic matter.

- Surround each raised bed with crushed granite for easy access. (Note granite lasts much longer than gravel from basalt or other kinds of rock.) Having a dirt-free working area makes it easier to practice no-till gardening, and there is less strain on your back when weeding a raised bed.

- To further extend your growing season, add a cold frame or cloche to a raised bed to protect the vegetables from cold temperatures and frost. A *cold frame* is a simple bottomless box usually made out of cedarwood, such as 2x6s, 2x8s, or 2x10s, with a removable glass or plastic lid. The back or north side of the south-facing

frame should be about 6 inches taller (typically about 18 inches high) than the south side (typically about 12 inches high). A *tunnel cloche* consists of a frame made with aluminum or PVC tubing in the form of a half circle tunnel and covered with plastic drop cloth, 4- to 6-mil plastic, or greenhouse plastic on top, and simple clips such as binder clips to secure the plastic to the tubing.

- Choose vegetable varieties that are resistant to diseases and pests and are adapted to our cool, wet Northwest springs. I have had success with growing varieties of beans, beets, broccoli, carrots, fava beans, garlic, kale, lettuce, onions, parsley, peas, potatoes, squash, tomatoes, and zucchini, interspersed with a variety of herbs.

- To minimize depleting the soil of selected nutrients and the buildup of pests and diseases, regularly rotate your vegetable crops to different areas of the planting bed or, better yet, to different planting beds. The reason is that plants from the different plant families have somewhat different nutrient requirements and are attacked by different pests. Changing the nature of the plantings in a given soil area each season will allow the soil to replenish its nutrients and will slow down any specific pests.

- Using cover crops, which are planted in the fall to cover a field in winter, also helps sustain the soil, replenish its nutrients, and break pest and disease cycles. Cover crops reduce runoff, erosion, and leaching of nutrients; replace soil organic matter; and suppress weeds. Some cover crops supply nitrogen (legumes) and/or attract beneficial insects. One combination I like to plant in October is small-seeded fava bean (which is a nitrogen-fixing legume) with winter wheat. Both can be turned back into the soil in early spring.

For resources that provide detailed information about planting vegetable gardens, see Resources.

LAWNS

Lawns are everywhere, surrounding homes and commercial areas and making up golf courses and sports fields. They are generally fairly sterile monocultures, made up of European turf grasses that require high maintenance and resource inputs. You know the infamous lawn cycle: Plant the seeds, irrigate them or run the sprinkler, treat the

For a lawn, consider alternatives to traditional grass sod.

lawn with herbicides, fertilizers, and/or a fertilizer/herbicide "weed and feed" mix. Then, once the grass is grown, cut it with a gas-powered lawnmower, which probably has a two-cycle engine and releases fine particulate matter, carbon dioxide, carbon monoxide, as well as nitrogen oxides and other harmful volatile chemicals into the air. Repeat ad infinitum.

There are tons of reasons to give up our insidious lawn addiction. For one thing, the chemicals and herbicides needed for maintenance harm beneficial soil organisms. They also create polluted groundwater, which eventually travels from yards into streams and lakes and harms aquatic organisms. Weed-and-feed products cause the most trouble, because they are designed to be broadcast indiscriminately over the entire lawn, whether a weed problem exists or not. This approach violates the basic principles of integrated pest management

A mix of grasses and small broadleaf plants creates a low-maintenance meadow.

(IPM), which requires regular monitoring of pests to determine if and when treatments are needed, or an *action threshold* (see Chapter 9, Sustainable Care).

I don't want you to think that I'm anti-lawn. Lawns, especially when sustainably maintained, are certainly preferable to barren ground or impervious pavement. The trick is in the type of lawn you choose to have. I propose two possibilities: a self-sustaining meadow or a water-efficient lawn.

Self-Sustaining Meadow

Lawns with a healthy mix of grasses and broadleaf plants, or *dicots* (short for "dicotyledon") such as clover, English daisy, yarrow, Roman chamomile, and sweet alyssum, can form a self-sustaining yet ever-changing meadow plant community. If they benefit from solid maintenance practices and a judicious use of technology, these site-adapted plants can provide significant environmental benefits. Alternative lawns

- require less mowing and watering;
- don't need herbicides or fertilizer;
- trap and remove airborne and water pollutants;
- process carbon and produce oxygen;
- recharge groundwater;
- minimize dust and soil erosion;
- cool the air through evapotranspiration (the process by which water moves from the soil and plant leaves back into the atmosphere).

What's more, grass-dicot mixtures support a diverse microbial population and provide habitat for wildlife, particularly when complemented with a multilayered landscape of trees, shrubs, and groundcovers. And don't forget that lawns contribute to human joys such as playing Frisbee or having a summer twilight picnic.

Ideally, the grasses should blend well with one another as well as with the dicots. For example, you could use a noninvasive lawn-replacement mix of tough, drought-tolerant fine fescues, such as Chewing's fescue (*Festuca rubra* ssp. *commutata*) or sheep fescue (*Festuca ovina*), and dwarf perennial ryegrass like winter ryegrass (*Lolium perenne*), along with a clover cultivar, such as white clover (*Trifolium repens*). Clover's roots happen to fix and hold nitrogen, thereby eliminating the need for additional fertilizers to feed the grasses. Clover is also a great source of nectar for bees. A mix of this kind is appropriate for cool or temperate marine climates, and it requires minimal irrigation and little or no fertilizer once established. Furthermore, it can tolerate relatively infertile and shady planting sites and resist common turf diseases.

In a city, successfully establishing a meadow of grasses and dicots from seed will require proper site selection and considerable site and soil preparation. During the first 3 years, you will need to perform vigilant weed control, monitoring, and strident maintenance in order to prevent the invasion of annual, biennial, and perennial weedy species. Later, you'll need to be on the lookout for the emergence of unwanted shrub and tree seedlings. The practicality of this approach depends on the characteristics of the specific

Clover and other dicots mixed with grasses form a nice lawn but will require vigilant maintenance the first few years.

Traditional lawns are so yesterday. If planted with the right seed, lawns do not need to be mowed regularly.

site and the amount and kind of aggressive weedy species present at nearby sites.

Water-Efficient Lawn

Another way to plant a lawn that will use fewer resources is to focus on grasses that need very little water, and to plant in a pattern that allows you to irrigate effectively. To make it easier to maintain your lawn, plan the lawn zone in a simple geometric shape, such as a square or rectangle. Avoid odd shapes or narrow strips—this will make it easier to mow and provide more flexibility in irrigation.

If you want to use the more commonly used underground sprinklers with pop-up heads, it may be hard to get complete and even water coverage, and some areas could end up being overwatered while others are underwatered, even when using variable arc nozzles. However, the newer low-volume subsurface drip lines made for lawns and placed underground are better suited for odd-shaped areas and are the most water-efficient way to water your lawn. For more on irrigation systems and practices, see Chapter 7, Water.

The type of grass seed mix you use is a major determinant of how much you will need to water your lawn. Grass mixes for the Pacific Northwest west of the Cascades usually are cool-season grasses containing perennial ryegrass, fine fescues, tall fescues, and bent grasses. Lawns east of the Cascades predominantly contain Kentucky bluegrass, often with some fine fescues. Unfortunately these lawns are high maintenance, requiring a lot of water and fertilizer.

- Perennial rye is a drought-tolerant and wear-tolerant bunchgrass.
- Fine fescues (Chewing's, creeping red, sheep, and hard fescue) are adaptable to poor, dry soils; they are shade tolerant but not suitable for heavy-use areas.
- Tall fescue is heat and drought resistant and somewhat shade tolerant.

LAWN MAINTENANCE TIPS

- Use an electric mulching mower or a push mower to eliminate the production of harmful pollutants (see Chapter 6, Sustainable Materials and Energy Choices, for more on environmentally friendly equipment).
- Leave the trimmings from a mulching lawnmower in place to provide nitrogen to the soil and food for beneficial soil organisms, and to reduce the need for fertilization.
- Irrigate deeply but infrequently in summer to encourage deep roots. Summers with little or no rain may require that you irrigate drought-tolerant grasses biweekly, or even once a week during the hottest part of the summer.
- Add about ½ inch of compost to the lawn in the fall. This can reduce stormwater runoff by up to 50 percent.
- Aerate and reseed the lawn to sustain dense turf and control weeds. A soil aeration machine (which you can rent) removes plugs of grass from the lawn, which allows air, water, and nutrients to penetrate to the grass's roots. Aerate in early spring or fall when the soil is moist. Aeration is needed when the lawn becomes compacted or there is buildup of dead grass or lawn thatch. Reseed the lawn in spring or fall when the lawn becomes thin or has bare spots.
- If needed occasionally to keep the lawn healthy, apply just enough of a slow-release nitrogen fertilizer in the fall to prevent yellowing and promote dense turf.
- For dealing with lawn pests, use the least toxic chemical control with the least non-target impact only as a method of last resort, after cultural, physical, mechanical, or biological controls have been tried and proved ineffective.

As you can see, even an optimized lawn takes considerable maintenance. So, downsizing your lawn or eliminating it entirely may save you some blood, sweat, and tears. This could also free up space for more environmentally friendly site-adapted native and nonnative plants. Use the open, sunny locations occupied by lawns for flowers, shrubs, vegetable beds, or fruit trees instead.

GRASSES TO AVOID

Kentucky bluegrass is poorly adapted to the wet and mild winters of the western Pacific Northwest and susceptible to diseases associated with cool, wet weather, and it does poorly in partial or full shade. To have a low-water-use lawn, do not include Kentucky bluegrass in your seed mix. Annual grasses are also not recommended.

- Bent grasses are not tolerant of heat or drought but are somewhat shade tolerant.
- Kentucky bluegrass is neither shade nor drought tolerant and its root system is relatively shallow compared to many other cool-season grasses.
- You can include some grasses native to the western Cascade region in your grass mix, such as creeping red fescue (*Festuca rubra*), western fescue (*Festuca occidentalis*), or blue wild rye (*Elymus glauca*). You may also wish to add low-growing, drought-tolerant herbaceous perennials to your grass mix.

For the western Pacific Northwest, it's fine to plant grass seed in the fall, in September and October. Alternatively, you can plant in April or early May when the soil is still moist. In the eastern Pacific Northwest, seeding conditions are more favorable in the spring after the soil temperature has reached 50°F. The site selected should be fairly level, with a slope of 10 percent or less. Ideally, the lawn should slope at least 1–5 percent away from your home or other buildings. Before planting, you need to prepare the site and soil. Here's a look at the whole process:

1. Take out the old lawn or other vegetation, and loosen the soil down to 8 inches by tilling or using a spading fork. Remove rocks and roots.

2. To determine what amendments your soil may need, do a soil test as described in Chapter 3. Oftentimes you can improve the properties of the soil by placing 3 inches of compost on top of the soil and then mixing it into the soil to a depth of 8 inches. As Northwest soils are usually acidic, it is sometimes necessary to raise the soil pH to a more optimal range, between 6 and 7.5 (for how to do this see Chapter 3, The Living Soil).

3. Once the soil has been properly prepared for your lawn, rake it smooth. Spread the seed at the rate recommended for the specific seed mix chosen (you can spread the seed by hand for small areas or use a broadcast spreader for larger areas). To aid in getting an even seed covering, distribute half the seeds by walking over the area in parallel lines. Then spread the remaining half while walking in a

direction at a right angle to the initial direction. For even coverage, you may need to seed the edge areas by hand.

4. To ensure good seed-to-seed contact to improve germination, very gently rake the seeds and then pass over the whole surface with a roller.

5. Moisten the seeds and cover them with a light dusting of fine compost.

6. Keep the seed and soil moist to a depth of 1–2 inches by gently spraying the seed several times a day.

7. As the seedlings begin to grow, in 2–3 weeks, reduce the watering frequency but moisten the soil to a greater depth. After 6–8 weeks you may add a slow-release fertilizer.

8. Once the seedbed is established, water the grass to the bottom of the roots, a depth of 6–8 inches, or about ¾–1 inch of water.

9. During the warmest and driest periods, water once a week. During other periods you can water less frequently.

CHAPTER CHECKLIST

☐ Select ornamental plants for four-season interest and that provide food and shelter and nesting resources for pollinators and other wildlife.

☐ Create multilayered landscapes with site-adapted and habitat-enhancing trees, shrubs, and groundcovers of multiple species that provide horizontal and vertical complexity and have different functions.

☐ Incorporate native edible plants and annual crops to add functionality to your garden.

☐ Create a more sustainable lawn, or convert as much of it as you can to other plantings.

6

SUSTAINABLE MATERIALS
AND ENERGY CHOICES

Up until this point in the book, we have discussed how to create healthy soil and plant site-appropriate plants that will contribute to the vitality of your yard. However, another large piece of building a sustainable garden is how you manage energy. The act of building a garden itself uses energy, much of it the sweat-and-elbow-grease kind. But sometimes other kinds are required, some of which might involve making a choice between the usual fossil fuels and more alternative sources, or between shiny new products and ones that have seen better days but are perfectly functional.

Besides choosing plants knowledgeably and thoughtfully, designing and maintaining your landscape with an eye to limiting energy and material use can reduce the urban heat island and the generation of greenhouse gases. Replacing one gasoline lawnmower with an electric or a push one may sound insignificant, but when you combine that with other pieces of environmentally friendly equipment, reused and recycled hardscape and fencing materials, and conserved water—and consider the scale of each person reading this book doing the same—your actions can have a big impact on preserving the earth's resources.

OPPOSITE: *Old materials are repurposed to form an ornamental wall collage.*

Using a manual lawnmower is good exercise and reduces the production of greenhouse gases and volatile organic chemicals.

ENVIRONMENTALLY FRIENDLY EQUIPMENT

Although alternatives are becoming more popular and easier to access, landscape equipment is still primarily powered by gasoline. Yard care tools like weed eaters, lawnmowers, and blowers might seem small, but they generate a lot of carbon dioxide, carbon monoxide, nitrogen oxides, and other smog-forming volatile organic chemicals. The use of gasoline lawnmowers on acres and acres of turf grass is undoubtedly the worst culprit.

Use manual garden equipment when you can. Not only is this the most environmentally friendly course of action, but you'll also be getting a good workout! Besides breathing fresh air and getting some health-boosting exercise, being outside in your environment and doing the hard but worthwhile work is what gardening is all about. A manual hedge trimmer and a real push mower do the job just fine.

Or you can lower petroleum use and greenhouse gas emissions by using alternative fuels, such as biodiesel or compressed natural gas, or electricity to power your lawnmower. While propane-powered lawnmowers are becoming available for commercial landscapers, smaller and more economical models are not yet available for residential homeowners. The good news is that you can buy both plug-in and cordless electric mowers. On the plus side, they don't produce any harmful emissions and they make less noise, but plug-in mowers can be a little harder to use since they require an electric outlet within roughly 100 feet of the grass you need to cut, and you will have to drag that electric cord around. A battery-operated mower can readily work for lawns that are too far from a plug.

For other landscape equipment—such as weed trimmers, hedge trimmers, leaf blowers, lawn edgers, and saws—a wide variety of electric plug-in and battery-powered equipment is now available. The voltage, size, and power of the battery varies; your selection will depend upon the specific use and the size of your pocketbook. The larger the voltage, ranging from 18 to about 60 volts, the bigger the tasks the equipment can handle.

For those of you in the market for a leaf blower, get one that is also able to vacuum and mulch your leaves, since mulched leaves are an excellent addition to the compost pile (while whole leaves tend to form mats that slow water flow within the pile).

SUSTAINABLE MATERIALS

Materials for building and maintaining your garden, like everything else, have a whole life cycle, from discovery to decomposition. First, the raw material must be extracted, then transported to a facility and processed in many steps and stages into a product. Then the product must do its job for however long it lasts and with all its necessary maintenance, through initial use and reuse to its reincarnated form, which is the percentage of it that can be recycled to make something else. Finally, at the end of usefulness comes disposal—whether to decompose in a landfill or behind your garage.

All of the energy employed to extract, transport, create, use, and dispose of the material is called *embodied energy*. When you select a material, whether that be wood for

GOING SOLAR

Of course, even electric landscape equipment can contribute to air pollution, as many electric power plants produce harmful pollutants, particularly if they burn coal. One way to escape the cycle is to use solar energy to generate electricity in your home. For more information about using solar energy, consult the following resources:

- American Solar Energy Society (ASES): www.ases.org
- The Washington chapter of ASES, Solar Washington: www.solarwa.org
- The Oregon chapter, Solar Oregon: www.solaroregon.org
- A similar organization in British Columbia, the BC Sustainable Energy Association: www.bcsea.org
- DSIRE: The Database of State Incentives for Renewables & Efficiency, maintained by the North Carolina Clean Energy Technology Center, provides information on federal, state, and local solar incentives across the country (www.dsireusa.org).

Plenty of repurposed old materials can add an element of whimsy to the garden.

a yard fence, concrete pavers for a patio, or large stones for a wall, alongside its cost and quality weigh its impact on the environment and human health.

The underlying goal is to minimize the depletion of nonrenewable resources, the degradation of ecosystems, and the disruption of ecosystem services. Thus, wise selection—including using reused or recycled material to avoid the extraction of virgin material—can help to reduce energy and resource consumption. It can go a long way toward decreasing greenhouse gas emissions and the amount of materials sent to landfills. To assist you in making wise choices for products used in your yard, consult the search-able interactive online directory that is part of the Grow Smart, Grow Safe program (available at www.oregonmetro.gov/tools-living /yard-and-garden-problems/make-sure -your-garden-product-safe) to find the least hazardous products and practices for a productive, safe, and healthy yard.

Consider Embodied Energy

Ask the following questions to assess a given material's sustainability.

- Is it widely available?
- Is it renewable or can it be regenerated?
- What percentage of it is recycled?
- What percentage of it can be recycled?
- How long will it last?

- Can it be reused?
- Does it require a lot of maintenance?
- Can it be maintained without toxic chemicals?
- Is it extracted, harvested, and manufactured as close as possible to your site?

There are two more questions, which may be more or less impossible to answer. Still, I believe they are worth considering: First, how much energy and water is needed to extract, transport, process, distribute, and dispose of the material? And second, how much waste material is generated to make it?

Let's consider the embodied energy of two well-established materials: natural granite stone and concrete. In the Pacific Northwest, natural granite is widely available because West Coast mountain ranges have lots of it. Granite can be used over and over again and will last a very long time. Once it is used to make a wall or stone path, it is durable and requires minimal maintenance. However, it does take energy to extract the rock at the local quarry or take it out of the local mountains, transport it to a facility and process it there, and then move the rock to your home. Still, overall, granite can be considered a sustainable material.

As for concrete, it is energy-intensive to make—a great deal of carbon dioxide emissions are generated during the process—and transport. But its raw materials—limestone, for example—are widely available locally. Depending on the concrete's use, it may require sealing, and over time it is prone to

crack, but it is usually durable and long lasting. More and more concrete is being recycled today, and it can be reused in alternate applications such as crushing it to serve as base material for roads. In conclusion, concrete is not as sustainable as natural stone, but improvements in the manufacturing process have the potential to make this most ubiquitous building material more sustainable.

Reduce, Reuse, Recycle

When building a landscape, consider every day a Buy Nothing Day. This holiday is a spinoff of Black Friday, the day after Thanksgiving, when Americans are encouraged to

This old wheelbarrow was headed to the dump when a neighbor saw it and asked if he could turn it into a portable flower bed.

LEFT: *Scrap metal I-beams welded into rectangular shapes and filled with gravel create garden steps.* **RIGHT:** *Tumbled glass mixed with gravel adds a decorative element to a walkway.*

get in fistfights over sale-priced electronics at superstores. Black Friday has been co-opted by anticonsumerists and "rebranded" as Buy Nothing day when people choose to, well, buy nothing. Here are two ways in which you might consider applying it to your landscape project (it's really not all that hard):

1. Divert material from the waste stream by reusing or salvaging material found on site or from local landscapes and buildings. You can often find salvaged plants and stone, along with used lumber, brick, glass, broken concrete, and metal, in areas that are being newly developed. Get a little creative in how you adapt these materials for your garden, with little or no processing. You can reduce maintenance and replacement costs by selecting materials that, by their continued existence, have proven to be long lasting, durable, and low maintenance.

2. Use locally sourced, recycled materials that have been reprocessed to create a new product or new materials with a high percentage of recycled content. Whenever possible, buy locally sourced material to reduce transportation, support the local economy, and give a sense of place.

Salvaged, recycled, or locally sourced materials such as those listed below can be used in a variety of ways to make attractive, novel, environmentally friendly landscapes.

Brick, Concrete, Stone

- Broken pieces of concrete, found at construction sites in your neighborhood, can become outdoor walls and benches.

Artfully placed scrap metal forms a creative border alongside a patio of reclaimed bricks and concrete.

- Reclaimed bricks or factory rejects sourced locally can be laid on a sand base and used for walkways and patios that will be both durable and permeable to water.
- Salvaged concrete pavers can be used for driveways, patios, and walkways. If placed properly on permeable material, the spaces between them allow water to pass through.
- Locally sourced ⅜- or ⅝-inch washed rock can be the base for relatively flat garden paths, with crushed granite for the top layer.
- Natural granite stepping stones can be used for steeper portions of the garden.

PAINTS, SEALANTS, COATINGS

Select paints, sealants, and coatings that contain minimal environmental hazards and emit low levels of volatile organic compounds (VOCs). VOCs are commonly released from paints, sealers, stains, adhesives, and pesticides, but many other products can emit VOCs. To avoid them, learn the VOC content of the materials and products you plan to purchase, use water-based instead of petroleum-based solvents, and select products that meet the Green Seal standard.

Solar lights are an energy-efficient way to light up a landscape.

Lumber

- Discarded cedar lumber can be used to make a planter bed, a tree house door, or a potting shed.
- Nontoxic materials high in recycled content can work for decks, railings, outdoor furniture, and fences. Because of our wet winters, recycled wood generally does not last very long unless it contains toxic preservatives. Salvaged disease-resistant wood such as cedar or redwood is a better choice but is less likely to be available. Wood-plastic composite made from recycled plastics and wood by-products may be more durable than wood but may undergo discoloration and needs to be cleaned regularly. Furthermore, the wood portion of the composite may be susceptible to mold or mildew, while the plastic may undergo UV degradation and could contain toxic material such as PVC. Perhaps a better choice is recycled plastic lumber made out of high-density polyethylene: durable, decay resistant, and requiring minimal maintenance, it can be used in many conventional lumber applications including decks, picnic tables, benches, and planters.
- If you want to purchase wood, make sure it's certified by the Forest Stewardship

Council, which ensures that the wood has been grown and harvested in a sustainable manner.

Repurposed Materials and Energy-Efficient Lighting

- Metal or glass castoffs can become a cold frame or greenhouse.
- By-products or discarded items can become garden walkways. For example, in Oregon, cracked hazelnut shells are available from Oregon Hazelnuts (see Resources), and you can source wood chips from tree-trimming companies throughout the Pacific Northwest. However, these materials will decompose in 4 to 5 years and need to be replaced.
- Use efficient solar, low-voltage, and LED lighting fixtures in buildings and landscapes.
- For sources of recycled and salvaged materials, see Resources. It's also worth taking the time to peruse Craigslist or the Freecycle Network. Note: When you discover that a material truly has reached the end of its usefulness, please dispose of it in the most environmentally sound manner available.

CHAPTER CHECKLIST

- ☐ Use environmentally friendly equipment, like electric lawnmowers or hand tools.
- ☐ For sustainable materials, you should consider the embodied energy of each material you bring into the yard.
- ☐ Buy less!
- ☐ Purchase recycled and salvaged materials.

7

WATER

To sustain a landscape, we must have water; to have a *sustainable* landscape, we must *conserve* water. For most of us in the Pacific Northwest, a seemingly endless supply of water is just a faucet away. But continued population growth, along with hotter and drier summers and decreasing snowpack, ups the demand for the limited surface water and groundwater available in summer, which must produce hydroelectric power, provide sufficient water in our streams for fish, irrigate our farms, and still provide drinking water and other water needs for the population. Water is a valuable and limited resource, and we must treat it as such by doing our best to imitate the natural water cycling that has supported life on Earth for billions of years.

LOW-WATER-USE PLANTS

The plants you select for your landscape largely determine how much water you will need for your garden. To conserve water, it is important to primarily choose plants that can withstand long periods without it, and that hold on to what little water they receive longer than most other plants. You can usually find some of these water-conserving, drought-tolerant plants, such as shore pine, tall Oregon grape, and Pacific wax myrtle, right in your own backyard. These are plants native to the region that are adapted to dry summers, wet mild winters, and local native soils, and they require little supplemental water once established. They have the added bonus of being more resistant to local pests and diseases and don't require additional fertilizer.

OPPOSITE: *A rain barrel can be both practical and attractive.*

A hydrozone from the author's garden containing sedum, lavender, salvia, penstemon, and columbine, requires little or no supplemental watering.

Trees and woody shrubs are generally good at conserving water because they can store water in their trunks and roots. Other drought-tolerant plants have thick, waxy leaves and/or small or deeply divided leaves. For example, conifers generally are quite drought tolerant, with their waxy cuticles and small leaves.

The plant list of shrubs and perennials in Chapter 5, Ornamentals and Edibles, is weighted toward drought-tolerant and low-water-use plants. Start with plants flagged as drought tolerant and then go on to other resources. For further information about drought-tolerant plants for the Pacific Northwest, see Resources.

Other site-appropriate, water-wise plants for the Northwest region include plants from parts of the world that have a Mediterranean-type climate like the Northwest, with little rainfall (less than 1 inch per month) from July through September. Some plants from east of the Cascade mountains (where there may be only ½ inch of rain per month during July and August) and hardy plants from arid portions of the world, such as parts of New Zealand or Australia, may be appropriate west of the Cascades, provided your soil has excellent drainage and the correct exposure.

Drought-tolerant species must be planted in healthy soil—rich in organic matter with good infiltration and the water-holding capacity to withstand extended dry periods (see Chapter 3, The Living Soil).

HYDROZONES

When building your garden, plant like with like. This means dividing the garden into *hydrozones*, or areas organized based on the water requirements of the plants, the type of soil, the wind, and the sun exposure. Doing so while also planting layered landscapes is a fun endeavor, much like solving a jigsaw puzzle. Creating these different zones allows you to use water more efficiently, helping you to avoid extra labor and migraine-inducing water bills.

To get started, you want to separate your garden into areas that will require regular irrigation, those that require reduced irrigation, and those that require very limited or no irrigation. You can do this by dividing your garden into lawn, perennial flower borders, shrub beds, and mixed beds containing drought-tolerant species.

Assuming there is about 200 square feet to fill (see Hydrozone Planting Plan next page), nine different plants are more than adequate to fill the space, since it is visually best to limit the different types of perennials in your design and plant the same perennial in clusters in odd numbers. Plant the smaller peren-

nials at the front of the border and the larger in the back. To make the border appear more naturalistic and informal, avoid planting in straight lines. Instead, make gentle curves for the edges of the planting bed.

The mature plant width determines the spacing of your plant. Thus, if your mature plant width is 2 feet, you will want to space your plants 2 feet apart or a little less. If this same plant is on the edge of the border, place the center of the plant at least 1 foot from the edge of the border. Balance the delicate-, moderate- and coarse-textured plants in this border.

From this list of plants, I suggest planting two clusters of five of the groundcover cranesbill in front of the border, one on the left corner and the other on the right. Next to these clusters, place two clusters of three of the iris. In the center of the border, group seven pineapple lilies in the form of an upside-down triangle. In the back of the border, locate two clusters of five evening primrose, one in the left corner and one in the right corner. One Joe Pye weed next to each of these clusters of evening primrose adds interest. Fill the rest of the back of the border with two clusters of three bee balm.

To irrigate this border, you could use small pop-up sprinklers with a spray span of 5 feet or the width of the border, but water would be lost through evaporation, and watering the foliage can make plants susceptible to disease. Therefore, drip irrigation is the most efficient way to water this border.

This is just an example, to illustrate principles to follow in designing your own hydrozone. Coming up with planting plans is the fun part of gardening—now it's your turn to get those creative juices going.

BEST WATERING PRACTICES

Best watering practices begin with *when* you plant: Planting in fall is better than planting in spring, particularly in climates with dry summers. The roots of fall-planted vegetation

HYDROZONE PLANTING PLAN FOR A PERENNIAL BORDER

Let's say you want to plant a perennial flower border in either full sun or partial shade, using plants that will require some supplemental water, particularly during the warm, dry days of July and August. Assuming you have already prepared the organic-rich, loamy soil for your planting bed and selected a border approximately 5 feet wide and 40 feet long behind your lawn in the backyard, begin to pick out herbaceous perennials that you like and that will need some supplemental water to look good. Make a note of their height and width, form, texture, and bloom time and color. To help you get started, I've picked out nine plants with similar water needs and a variety of characteristics and organized them into a sample arrangement. As I like blues, lavenders, and yellows, I used these colors for a pattern in this border.

PLANT	SIZE	FORM	TEXTURE	BLOOM TIME	FLOWER COLOR
Bee balm (*Monarda didyma* 'Violet Queen')	2–4 ft. tall x 2–3 ft. wide	Upright	Moderate	Summer	Lavender
Blazing star (*Liatris spicata*)	2–4 ft. tall x 1–2 ft. wide	Upright	Moderate	Summer	Purple and white
Columbine (*Aquilegia chrysantha*)	1–3 ft. tall x 0.5–2 ft. wide	Upright	Delicate	Late spring and summer	Yellow
Cranesbill (*Geranium cantabrigiense* 'Biokovo')	6–8 in. tall x 24 in. wide	Groundcover	Delicate	Late spring and summer	White
Dwarf Joe Pye weed (*Eutrochium dubium* 'Baby Joe')	2.5 ft. tall and wide	Upright	Coarse	Late summer and fall	Purple
Evening primrose (*Oenothera fruticosa* 'Sundrops')	1.7 ft. tall and wide	Groundcover	Delicate	Summer	Yellow
Iris (*Iris setosa*)	1–2 ft. tall and wide	Mound	Moderate	Late spring and summer	Blue and purple
Pineapple lily (*Eucomis comosa* 'Sparkling Burgundy')	2–3 ft. tall x 2 ft. wide	Mound	Moderate	Summer	Purple
Threadleaf coreopsis (*Coreopsis verticillata* 'Zagreb')	1.5 ft. tall and wide	Groundcover	Delicate	Summer and fall	Yellow

A sprinkler system might water areas that don't need to be watered, particularly in windy conditions, and significant amounts of water can be lost through evaporation in sunny conditions on hot days.

continue to grow until cold weather arrives, establishing their root systems better than warmer-season plantings and ultimately requiring less water.

Like a newborn baby, initially the plants and their needs run the show—water them when they need it rather than on a fixed schedule. For the 1 or 2 years it takes drought-tolerant or low-water-use plants to get established, they need deep watering at the root zone during dry periods. Some perennials and most annual flowers and vegetables will need some supplemental water during the dry summers. The best time to water is early in the morning, since this minimizes evaporation and gives the plants time to dry out before evening, lessening their vulnerability to harmful fungal pathogens.

Avoid watering during sunny or windy periods, since too much of the water evaporates to be efficient. Water slowly and deeply—but infrequently—to encourage deep root growth and increase drought resistance. However, how you water will depend on your soil type. For example, areas with clay soils—which let water in slowly, with an infiltration rate of approximately 0.1 inch per hour—may require multiple short run times whereby you water the area for no more than 5 to 10 minutes at a time, pause to allow the water to soak in, then irrigate the area again for another 5 to 10 minutes.

You can leave disease-free leaf litter on the ground in order to keep water where it is needed. Plus, leaf litter decomposes into mulch, which soaks up and then slowly

Sometimes it is practical to hand water just where you need it.

releases water and nutrients and helps control weeds. However, you'll want to clear away larger leaves that could smother small plants.

Unnecessary watering not only wastes a precious resource; it's also just bad gardening form. It makes plants more susceptible to pests and disease, facilitates the growth of weeds, enhances erosion and washes away soil nutrients, and increases the need for fertilizers and pesticides. This is where an efficient irrigation system comes in.

Water-Thrifty Irrigation

If you have low-water and drought-resistant plants and you plant in the fall, you can avoid putting in an irrigation system altogether. But in general a sustainable garden needs a well-designed and efficient irrigation system that can provide uniform water coverage and optimal application rates. This will maximize water infiltration and minimize runoff.

There are some wonderful new technologies and smart irrigation-control systems that can help you manage your water usage. Below, I discuss the pros and cons of three types of irrigation systems; use this information to decide which is the best fit for your site and plants.

Once an irrigation system is operational, inspect it regularly to make sure there are no leaks or defective heads. To avoid overwatering, ensure that the type of irrigation, coverage, and schedule matches the plant types, soil type and depth, and sun exposure in each hydrozone.

Hand Irrigation

A practical approach for getting your waterwise plants established is hand watering using your garden hose, with a wand or nozzle attached to the end to control the flow. Assuming you planted in the fall, your plants will already have a fairly good root system to help them through their first summer. However, they still will need watering during at least the first summer.

Hand watering allows you to water only the plants you want, right at the root zone, with just the needed amount of water.

You can adjust the rate at which water is added based on how the soil is absorbing the water. For clay soils or slopes with slow water infiltration rates, it's a good idea to make a small berm around each plant at planting time to prevent runoff. You may need to add water to the soil inside the berm multiple times in one watering session to ensure that the soil is saturated down through the root zone. After watering, try pushing a spade or soil probe into the soil to determine the depth that the moisture reached. If watering is done carefully, you can avoid wetting the foliage, and minimize runoff and weed germination.

There is little expense in this approach except for a hose and nozzle. However, it does require considerable time, and you have to drag the hose around your garden. For me, though, watering my "new babies" in the early morning hours as the sun comes up, while listening to the sounds of nature, is a relaxing, rewarding experience.

Drip Irrigation

Wherever practical, use drip irrigation in planting beds, as drip irrigation applies water uniformly and precisely where you want it to go, minimizing surface evaporation and eliminating spray blockage by foliage. Drip irrigation requires an outdoor faucet to supply the drip system with water. The water can be turned off or on manually but is usually controlled with a timer. The tubing is placed around the plants at the soil surface and covered with mulch to help retain moisture and prevent sunlight from damaging it.

Drip irrigation has many advantages. The water is emitted slowly and directly into the soil near the plant roots so this approach evenly distributes moisture; minimizes water loss from evaporation, wind, and runoff; lessens erosion; reduces weed germination in the areas not watered; and keeps water from getting on foliage, thereby minimizing diseases such as mildew or mold. Drip irrigation is particularly useful for efficiently watering containers, vegetable beds, and shrubbery in your planting beds.

With the drip system it is not easy to see how much water is being applied, so you must check the emitters and soil regularly (every week or so) to make sure they are

DIY SYSTEM FOR A RAISED VEGETABLE GARDEN

You can purchase a drip irrigation kit from your local home improvement store, and setting it up is relatively easy and inexpensive. The components include

- a backflow preventer, which prevents contamination of your potable water;
- a pressure regulator to lower the pressure to 25–30 psi, an acceptable level for the drip tubing;
- a filter to remove sediment;
- a tubing adapter, which allows joining of different-size tubing;
- ½-inch tubing for attaching to the adapter, with or without ¼-inch lateral tubing;
- emitters that attach to the tubing and release water drop by drop (about ½–2 gallons per hour);
- a timer.

Follow the instructions enclosed with the kit. Supplemental to those, the following instructions walk you through the steps in setting up a drip irrigation system for a raised vegetable garden.

- Connect the backflow preventer to the outdoor faucet.
- Attach the Y-valve to the backflow preventer. There should be shutoff valves on each side of the Y.
- Attach the pressure regulator to one side of the Y-valve.
- Attach the timer to the pressure regulator.
- Install the filter at the end of the pressure regulator.
- Add PVC connector to the filter.
- Run ¾-inch PVC pipe to the raised bed.
- Attach a ½- to ¾-inch adapter to the ¾-inch PVC pipe.
- Attach ½-inch drip tubing.
- Place the ½-inch tubing along each plant row.
- Punch holes in the tubing where plants will be, and insert drip emitters that emit 2 gallons per hour into the holes.
- Cover the tubing with 2–3 inches of mulch.

NOTE: Always drain your drip irrigation system before winter.

An automatic sprinkler in a raised bed

not clogged or that there is no build up of pressure in the tubing. Also, the system must be periodically flushed to prevent mineral buildup within the tubing. A system that is not delivering the proper amount of water to the roots can cause shallow root growth, poor root development, and even the death of plants.

Automatic Sprinkler System

Automatic sprinkler systems are appropriate for large open areas, such as lawns. The layout of the sprinklers and the type of sprinkler head can vary widely and still achieve even water distribution and minimize runoff. The essential components of an automatic sprinkler include

- a dedicated water source;
- a backflow preventer device;
- a programmable controller/timer for scheduling the watering day(s), start times, and duration of watering for each zone;
- valves for turning off and on each zone of sprinklers, along with low-voltage wire for attaching to the solenoid in the valve;
- valve boxes for access, as the valves are usually placed underground;
- a manual shutoff valve at each zone;
- PVC tubing for transporting the water to the sprinkler heads.

A smart controller also can have on-site rain and soil sensors that automatically turn off the system when irrigation is not needed.

There are broadly two types of sprinklers used in residential settings today: rotor sprinklers and fixed-spray sprinklers. In the first type, gear-driven rotor nozzles stream out water while rotating at the same time. They are used for irrigating large areas, since a single rotor can throw water between 15 and 35 feet. The gear-driven rotor head is generally better for watering slopes and soils high in clay content, because it distributes the water at a lower rate than a fixed-spray head. Fixed-spray heads are appropriate for small to medium-size areas (width of 18 feet or less) and areas with tight curving edges. They are usually pop-up and are placed underground so they are nearly invisible when not in use. These spray heads can distribute water in a full circle, half circle, or quarter circle and be adjusted to a specific arc of water.

To estimate your sprinkler output, scatter coffee or soup cans throughout the lawn and capture the water during irrigation. Measure the depth of the water in each can, and take the average to get your sprinkler output. Here are some recommended levels:

- *Lawns:* Set the irrigation schedule so the lawn is soaked 6–10 inches deep through the root zone. To minimize runoff, do not water the lawn with more than 1 inch of water at a time.
- *Groundcovers:* Soak the soil down to 10–12 inches.
- *Shrubs:* Soak the soil down to around 24 inches (water at the drip line—the area directly under the outer circumference of the tree's or shrub's branches, where it sheds water).

- *Trees:* Soak down to 36 inches (water at the drip line).

The advantage of the automatic system is that it can be adjusted to run on any surface, the area doesn't need to be flat, and it can irrigate small or large areas automatically while you are sleeping. However, an automatic system is expensive to put in place and usually requires the advice of an irrigation professional to design it and assist in setting it up. Furthermore, this approach is less efficient than the drip system because water is lost due to evaporation and runoff. Also, sprinkler systems often water areas that don't need to be watered, particularly in windy conditions.

MINIMIZING POTABLE WATER USE

Freshwater shortages are becoming more common in urban communities because of population growth, reduced groundwater recharge, and wasteful consumption. As gardeners, we need to use much less potable (drinking) water to irrigate. Thus, the landscape should primarily depend upon precipitation and wastewater resources. Rainwater harvesting and using on-site nonpotable water from surplus or renewable sources, such as *graywater* or wastewater in your home, are two great ways you can minimize the use of potable water.

Graywater

Graywater is relatively clean water (without fecal contamination) from bathtubs, sinks, showers, and washing machines. From these sources, it is safe to use for irrigation, particularly if applied a few inches below the soil surface. Fortunately, rerouting graywater from the washing machine is a relatively simple DIY project, achievable by the average homeowner. For sources of information on how to do this, see Resources.

Few washing machine detergents are free of chemicals and sodium salts that are harmful to soils, but their numbers are growing. Bio Pac and Oasis make laundry detergents that are fine for graywater; Oasis's all-purpose cleaner and Dr. Bronner's Magic Soap are graywater-compatible detergents that can be used for washing dishes or hands. No matter how green a cleaning product is, though, *never use graywater to irrigate the vegetable garden.* Use it instead to water all the vegetation that you *won't* be eating.

Please note that the use of graywater for irrigation may require the approval of your municipality's public health department or may even be prohibited entirely in your city.

Rainwater

Most buildings and homes carry stormwater runoff from roofs to gutters and then to downspouts that direct the water to the city storm drain. This drain is often connected to the sewer system. Not only does this arrangement waste water that could be used more efficiently, it places significant strain on the sewer system during storm events and increases the likelihood of system overflows.

Rain barrels are an effective and easy way to conserve water.

Stormwater runoff—even from a residential roof, and especially from roadways—is a source of pollution that can significantly contribute to contamination of our streams, lakes, and bays.

On residential properties, rainwater harvesting is a relatively easy way to conserve water. Instead of going down into storm drains, stormwater is redirected into rain barrels, cisterns, or other containment systems, where it can be stored and used later

Use a screen to keep debris out of a rain barrel.

for irrigation or to flush toilets. Harvesting rainwater not only keeps rainfall on site, it also helps you save on municipal water bills and can provide water year-round, giving you a little wiggle room in water usage during droughts. Stormwater from roofs and other impervious surfaces, along with water in rain barrels and cisterns, can also be redirected into landscape stormwater-management features, such as rain gardens.

An average rain barrel holds about 55 gallons of water; a larger one can hold 90 gallons. It is relatively easy to install, takes up little space, is not expensive, and readily fills up with water. Here's how to set up a rain barrel:

1. Locate the rain barrel under a downspout (with a leaf screen) on a flat, solid base of poured concrete, concrete pavers, or blocks, 4 or more inches above ground level.

2. Cut a 4- to 6-inch hole in the top of the plastic cover; this will be the inlet.

3. Cover the inlet with a fine screen to keep out insects and debris.

4. Make sure the lid of the barrel is secure, to prevent children or animals from getting in.

5. Drill a 1-inch hole about 3 inches from the bottom, and install a drain valve or garden hose faucet.

6. Drill another 1-inch hole about 3 inches from the top, and screw a ¾-inch fitting into the hole to allow overflow.

7. Drill a 3- to 4-inch hole near the bottom of the barrel and install a cleanout plug.
8. To use your accumulated water, connect a garden hose to the faucet, directing the flow away from the house to a rain garden or similar place where the water can safely soak into the soil. If your rain barrel threatens to overflow, attach a garden hose to the fitting near the top, and direct the water to a safe overflow area away from the house.
9. Clean the tank out at least once a year to remove sediment from the bottom of the barrel.

To increase the rain barrel's water-holding capacity, you can link multiple barrels in a series, so that when the first barrel fills, the excess water will flow into the second barrel, and so on.

How do you know how many rain barrels you might need to install? An inch of rain on 1 square foot of roof yields just under $2/3$ gallon of water. A typical home with 1,000 square feet of roof will produce about 620 gallons of water, but about 15 percent of that is lost to evaporation or is spilled or splashed over the gutters. Therefore, 1 inch of rain will generate about 530 gallons of water coming through the downspouts. As the Pacific Northwest gets about 40 inches of rain a year, the downspouts of a typical home will channel about 21,200 (40 x 530) gallons of water per year. To collect it all, you would need to piggyback 385 rain barrels!

Luckily, it doesn't all come at once. During the summer months you will probably be using water from the rain barrel to irrigate the garden, and as little as slightly more than a tenth of an inch of rain on 1,000 square feet of roof could fill the barrel up again. Thus, your rain barrel(s) could potentially be filled and emptied multiple times during the summer months (provided there are summer rains), when the water is needed most.

But rain barrels may not be the solution your situation calls for. For instance, what if you want to collect water to irrigate your lawn? Lawns are generally the biggest users of water, so let's calculate how much water your lawn is likely to need.

To make a conservative estimate, we will assume you have put in a more sustainable lawn using drought-tolerant grasses and one or more broadleaf herbaceous perennials. Assuming, then, that you will water the lawn once a week during the 6 weeks from mid-July through August, and every other week during the 14 weeks comprising May, June, half of July, and September, you will need to water a minimum of 13 times per year. To provide one inch of water and ensure that it gets through to the root zone, you need 0.62 gallon of water per square foot of lawn. That means that, for a 1,000-square-foot lawn (31.6 feet x 31.6 feet), each watering will require 620 gallons, for a total of 8,060 gallons (13 x 620) during one watering season. For conventional lawns you would undoubtedly water at least twice as often, needing at least 16,120 gallons

LEFT: *A permeable brick walkway* **RIGHT:** *Stormwater runoff from impervious driveways washes leaking oil from cars into our streams and waterways.*

(26 x 620). As you can see, to have a substantial impact on your irrigation needs you will need to increase your water-holding capacity. This brings us to the topic of cisterns.

A cistern can hold hundreds to thousands of gallons of water, so it is a better option if you want to store enough water to meet a significant portion of your landscape irrigation needs—and you have the space. Cisterns can be made of various materials, some strong and durable such as concrete or corrugated steel, and they can be installed below- or aboveground. For an aboveground cistern, molded plastic is a more affordable and common option; furthermore, aboveground tanks tend not to require a permit for digging. The

approach to installing a cistern is similar to that for a rain barrel; for specific information, visit www.seattle.gov/util/rainwise.

MINIMIZING STORMWATER RUNOFF

When water falls to the ground as rain, sleet, hail, or snow, a few things can happen. If the ground is a "natural" surface such as a forest floor or open prairie, much of the water will be absorbed into the soil and/or taken up by plants, which then help to filter it before it continues on its way. What doesn't evaporate or go into the soil will become stormwater, running along the surface of the ground and ending up in rivers, streams, or other bodies of water.

In cities, a majority of the water that falls becomes stormwater. This is because most of the surfaces that were once pervious—another word for permeable—have been paved. Certain kinds of stone, brick, concrete, and asphalt are impervious surfaces, so when water lands on them it can't go down into the soil. Instead, it flows where gravity pulls it, gathering hydrocarbons, heavy metals, and other hazardous substances along the way and ending up in nearby lakes and streams. This is not ideal, for obvious reasons.

Two ways you can contain stormwater runoff on your property, diverting it from the storm drain and thus out of waterways, are to install permeable pavements and build a rain garden.

Permeable Pavement

Impervious surfaces should be minimized wherever possible. If you have an unused driveway or other such wasted impermeable surface, consider getting rid of it (and recycling the materials; see Chapter 6, Sustainable Materials and Energy Choices).

Finding alternatives, such as permeable or porous pavement, is an important *integrated management practice* (IMP) for low-impact development. As these systems allow water to infiltrate through the material or between the pavers, they help facilitate stormwater infiltration, meaning that the stormwater can be more evenly dispersed. This, in turn, helps to maintain groundwater levels, as well as the interface between land and riparian areas (rivers and streams). Enhanced infiltration

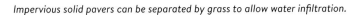

Impervious solid pavers can be separated by grass to allow water infiltration.

also prevents wells and springs from going dry, reduces the quantity of water being sent to holding ponds (thereby freeing up excavated areas that had previously served as holding ponds), can capture and help remove harmful pollutants before they enter local waterways, provides treatment and storage of water for possible reuse, and reduces the cost of the regional stormwater-management system.

Permeable pavement systems include

- porous asphalt and pervious concrete;
- impervious solid pavers with joints that are filled with permeable aggregates, such as interlocking concrete pavers that allow water through the joints;
- plastic (often made with recycled plastic) or concrete grid systems that have openings filled by soil planted with grass or low-maintenance groundcovers, called "open-celled paving grids."

Permeable asphalt and concrete require specialty contractors for installation. Permeable asphalt is fine for walkways and provides an even surface for wheelchair use. However, it wears out faster than concrete pavers and is expensive to install. Permeable concrete can be used for driveways and high volumes of traffic and will last for many years, but it is energy intensive to make and expensive to install.

Interlocking concrete pavers and open-celled paving grids, on the other hand, can be installed by a homeowner without professional assistance. They are durable, reusable, and particularly useful for patios, walkways, and driveways. They require that the site be excavated and prepared with an aggregate sublayer, and the final surface must be kept clean of debris and fine sediment. They are available in a variety of colors and styles. Open-celled paving grids are appropriate for low-use parking areas or walkways, provided they are on level ground. They require routine maintenance. A variety of these permeable paver systems can be purchased from your community's home improvement store.

Rain Gardens

A rain garden is a shallow landscape depression combined with vegetation and amended or designed soils to capture, absorb, and filter rainfall and stormwater from areas such as roofs, driveways, and the overflow from rain barrels and cisterns. Rain gardens help to manage the overall flow of water through the city by enhancing infiltration and *bioretention*—the process by which contaminants and sediments are removed from stormwater—and reducing stormwater, improving water quality, and adding beauty and value to neighborhoods and backyards. A rain garden is a relatively low-cost and easy way to get the stormwater on the gound surface to soak into the soil naturally, which prevents pollution from entering local wetlands and streams. A rain garden also has the added benefit of enhancing habitat for beneficial wildlife.

Rain gardens are usually installed on private property, and since they're smaller in scale than commercial or industrial bioretention facilities—typically 100 to 300 square feet—and for residential use, they do not generally require professional engineering like other bioretention facilities. Filled with a unique rain garden mix of compost, sandy soil, and screened sand, a rain garden holds water until it can soak into the ground. Then, through primarily herbaceous native plants that are able to withstand both very wet conditions and drought, the water is taken up and filtered. An overflow system near the surface prevents flooding, allowing water to escape to a safe place during heavy winter rains. Multiple small rain gardens joined together in a series or throughout a site can effectively supplement other stormwater-control measures.

Before you start digging, you need to decide whether you have an appropriate location and adequate space for a rain garden. Your site should be on fairly level land free of tree roots and utilities. You first want to consider how you will collect stormwater from your driveway or roof and direct it to your rain garden. For your rain garden, select a natural low area with good drainage (greater than 1 inch per hour). The size of the rain garden should be at least 10 percent of the impervious areas collecting the stormwater. For example, water directed from 1,000 square feet of roof requires a rain garden of at least 100 square feet. If the rain garden is placed in a site that drains poorly, I recommend an even larger rain garden.

This roadside rain garden helps manage stormwater runoff for the neighborhood.

How to Make a Rain Garden

The instructions below will help you learn the basics about building a rain garden, but in order to install a safe and approved rain garden in your yard, it's best to augment this information with other instruction.

First, consult with your county conservation district or local public utility. A number of conservation districts in Washington State, such as Kitsap, Snohomish, and Pierce counties, offer technical assistance.

Kitsap County also has an incentive rebate program that permits you to receive reimbursement for the costs of materials and installation. King County Conservation District offers technical and financial assistance for a variety of water-related purposes. There is also the 12,000 Rain Gardens program (www.12000raingardens.org), for the entire Puget Sound area, and the RainWise program (http://rainwise.seattle.gov/city /seattle/overview), which is a function of Seattle Public Utilities. For those interested in building a rain garden, 12,000 Rain Gardens offers resources, while RainWise offers rebates to qualified homeowners.

In Oregon, the East Multnomah Soil and Water Conservation District (www .emswcd.org) provides educational, technical, and (in some areas) financial assistance to landowners installing rain gardens. The West Multnomah Soil and Water Conservation District (www.wmswcd.org) provides guidance on best management practices to reduce stormwater runoff, erosion, and pollution.

For sources of further details about rain garden construction, see Resources.

There are a few basic steps to constructing a rain garden:

Select a location. Pick a low spot or shallow depression that drains well (ideally more than 1 inch per hour) and is away from the house, septic tank, drain field, underground utilities, bottom of a steep bank, root zone of existing trees, or water well.

Determine the garden's size and shape. The overall goal of the rain garden is to collect all the runoff and keep it on site. However, it is not mandatory that a single rain garden handle all the runoff; the more stormwater it can handle the better, but it is fine if your garden can accommodate only a portion of your site's stormwater.

- On a flat site, an egg-, crescent-, or kidney-shaped rain garden usually works well.
- On a sloping site, a long, narrow shape placed perpendicular to the slope works best.
- Residential rain gardens are typically 100 to 300 square feet in area.

Excavate and amend the soil. How deep to excavate the garden depends upon several factors: the *ponding* depth, or depth of the pooling water; the amount of soil mix you have; and the *overflow containment* depth, or the distance from the very top of the rain garden to the bottom of the overflow drain.

- For poor-draining soil, the total excavation depth would be from 24 to 42 inches, to make room for: 6 inches overflow containment + 6–12 inches ponding depth + 12–24 inches rain garden mix.
- If you have good-quality soil (without too much clay) and your soil drains more than 1 inch per hour, you can excavate to just 15 to 21 inches: 6 inches for overflow containment + 6–12 inches for ponding depth + 3 inches of compost tilled into

existing soil (instead of using a rain garden mix).

The excavation depth can be reduced somewhat if the rain garden is placed on a slight slope. Use soil from the uphill side of the rain garden to create a berm downhill on the edge of the overflow containment area. Make sure the bottom of the excavation is level by placing a carpenter's level on top of a straight board in the bottom of the excavation.

Rain garden soil mix typically contains 60 percent screened sand and 40 percent compost by volume. Alternatively, you could use 25 percent sandy loam, 45 percent screened sand, and 30 percent compost, which may provide better nutrients for your plants. You can either purchase this mix or create it on site.

Landscape your rain garden. Each rain garden has three hydrozones:

- Zone 1: The bottom of the rain garden, which is exposed to periodic flooding or standing water.
- Zone 2: The inside slopes, which are exposed to periodic wet soils during big storms.
- Zone 3: The drier perimeter.

Regardless of the hydrozone, all rain garden plants need to be able to tolerate extended dry periods. Select plants to match the environment. The plants below do well in Pacific Northwest rain gardens situated in full or partial sun.

OTHER BIORETENTION FACILITIES

Other types of bioretention facilities are much like rain gardens, except that they are engineered to infiltrate and treat a specific amount of stormwater and are commonly associated with commercial properties and public right-of-ways. Native plants are generally used and often mandated by cities for bioretention facilities. However, some nonnatives can function as well, if not better, for water absorption and filtration, as they are sometimes better adapted than natives to the novel conditions often found in urban areas.

Soil mixes for bioretention areas filter water rapidly enough to prevent the breeding of mosquitoes, but still slowly enough to allow for adequate removal of pollutants.

Zone 1

Henderson's checker mallow (*Sidalcea hendersonii*)
Indian rhubarb (*Darmera peltata*)
Iris (*Iris tenax*, *Iris douglasiana*)
Monkey flower (*Mimulus cardinalis*, *Mimulus guttatus*)
Moor grass (*Molinia caerulea* 'Variegata')
Red-twig dogwood (*Cornus sericea* 'Kelseyi')
Rush (*Juncus acuminatus*, *Juncus ensifolius*)
Sedge (*Carex obnupta*)

A soakage trench allows more water to return to the soil rather than becoming runoff.

Zone 2

Columbine (*Aquilegia formosa, Aquilegia chrysantha*)

Daylily (*Hemerocalis* sp.)

Douglas aster (*Symphyotrichum subspicatum*)

Dwarf tall Oregon grape (*Berberis aquifolium* 'Compacta')

Hardy geranium (*Geranium cantabrigiense* 'Biokovo')

Iris (*Iris tenax, Iris douglasiana*)

Sweet flag (*Acorus gramineus* 'Ogon')

Wallflower (*Erysimum* sp.)

Zone 3

Avens (*Geum triflorum*)

Beardtongue (*Penstemon pinifolius*)

Catnip (*Nepeta* x *faassenii* 'Walker's Low')

Flowering currant (*Ribes sanguineum*)

Hardy geranium (*Geranium macrorrhizum* 'Variegatum')

Stonecrop (*Sedum spathulifolium*)

Sunrose (*Helianthemum nummularium*)

Yarrow (*Achillea millefolium*)

Maintain the rain garden. Water your new rain garden plants during the dry summer months for 2 to 3 years until they are fully established. Apply several inches of mulch such as wood chips around your new plants annually, to keep the weeds from germinating and keep the soil moist. Regularly inspect the outlet and inlet, and remove any debris that may collect there.

Soakage Trench

In addition to rain barrels, a cistern, or a rain garden, another way to greatly reduce the amount of stormwater going to the city's drainage system is by directing water from your downspouts into a soakage trench. Dig a trench, and place perforated pipe in the bottom, surrounding it with $^3/_8$-inch or $^5/_8$-inch washed rock; larger river rock can be placed on the surface. Use 4-inch drain piping to carry water away from your downspout or rain barrel, safely away from your home, and into the soakage trench. The trench allows the runoff to soak into the soil, where it can recharge the groundwater. Any excess water not taken up by the soil can be directed to a rain garden.

For a soakage trench to be effective, it needs to be on fairly level ground, no more than a 15 percent slope, and away from tree roots and septic systems. You can have shallow-rooted plantings around it, but avoid plants with aggressive roots. To ensure that it does not get clogged, keep debris and sediment out of the trench and specifically out of the perforated pipe. Facilitate this by placing a silt basin between your drainpipe and the soakage trench, to filter out any sediment from your downspouts.

CHAPTER CHECKLIST

- ☐ Choose low-water-use plants.
- ☐ Arrange plants in hydrozones, or groupings with similar water needs.
- ☐ Install an irrigation system based on your site's needs to use water thriftily.
- ☐ Minimize potable water use.
- ☐ Reuse graywater.
- ☐ Collect rainwater in rain barrels or cisterns.
- ☐ Minimize stormwater runoff.
- ☐ Install permeable pavement.
- ☐ Build a rain garden.
- ☐ Make soakage trenches.

8

URBAN WILDLIFE
SANCTUARY

*H*abitat is the physical and biotic environment in which a species or organism lives, reproduces, obtains water and nutrients, and finds shelter. It can be as small as a planting box on a windowsill or as large as a city park or an entire mountain range. Regardless of the size of your garden, you can attract many kinds of wildlife and improve habitat for a large variety of species—and what happens in your yard and neighborhood has a major impact on local and regional biodiversity.

Most wildlife like the same things we do—tasty and nutritious snacks, clean water, a nice place to lay their weary heads and raise their offspring. Your yard can provide all those things. Insects, spiders, and amphibians love to roam a healthy bed of soil and mulch; birds look to trees, shrubs, and groundcover for seeds and berries, as well as places to build their nests. If you need a reason to leave old trees, standing dead trees (tree snags) that are not deemed a safety hazard, and old fallen logs in your yard, consider the fact that birds will love them: old trees' cavities provide perfect shelter for building nests and laying eggs, as well as a source of insects for food. Evergreen trees and shrubs, thickets of shrubs with thorns, and piles of brush or rocks provide safe places for wildlife to hide, get out of bad weather, or raise their young.

OPPOSITE: *Provide a water source to encourage year-round visits from birds, such as this Steller's jay.*

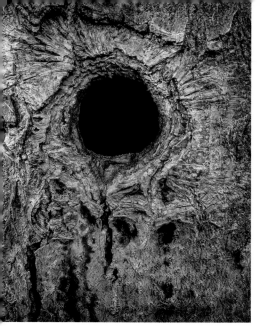 

LEFT: *Tree cavity for birds and other wildlife* RIGHT: *Plants with winter berries, like this juniper, will attract birds to your garden year round.*

BIRDS

When I replaced a dense patch of invasive Himalayan blackberry (*Rubus armeniacus*) with an array of native and nonnative plants, I saw a nearly fivefold increase in bird visitations to my garden. Anna's hummingbird is now a year-round resident, and other hummingbird species—with their remarkable acrobatics and glorious colors—are frequent visitors. Also, I now annually observe a veritable avian circus: the western bluebird, Steller's jay, chestnut-backed chickadee, black-capped chickadee, house finch, song sparrow, white-crowned sparrow, black-headed grosbeak, Bewick's wren, northern flicker, bushtit, yellow warbler, and American goldfinch all step into the ring at one point or another. All it took was a little spicing up of my plant mix to provide food and cover. The lists in Chapters 4 and 5 highlight plants that provide food and cover for birds.

Bird Feeders

To up your chances of solid bird-watching, install feeders in well-placed locations with plant cover nearby. To keep birds from flying into your picture window and killing themselves, it's best to place the feeder greater than 15 feet from the window or, alternatively, attach it directly to the window or less than 2 feet from it. Placing decals on your window also helps prevent birds from crashing into it. Some birds prefer to have shrubs or bushes near the feeder for potential shelter from prey, while other birds prefer to have it in an open area. Having feeders in both types of locations will attract the greatest variety of birds. It is important to clean your feeders

A male Anna's hummingbird on a contorted filbert.

and the areas around them every few weeks to prevent the spread of disease. They can be disinfected with a mixture of vinegar and water.

Because birds have different seed preferences, decide which kinds of birds you want to feed before you purchase birdseed. Many kinds of small birds, such as chickadees, jays, and nuthatches, love hulled sunflower seeds, which are a more manageable size than unhulled sunflower seeds and create less of a mess; however, they'll turn gummy if they get wet. Roasted peanut kernels, millet, and thistle are other seeds included in seed mixes. But while seed mixes may attract more kinds of birds to the feeder, more seed will get knocked to the ground as the birds pick through it to find the type they prefer. So, to avoid overcrowding, wasting seed, or attracting vermin, it is better not to use seed

mixes. Instead, set up multiple feeders, each with a different type of seed. You can plant sunflowers and millet in the garden to supply a source of these seeds for the birds to eat in winter.

Suet or fat is particularly attractive to insect-eating birds such as nuthatches and juncos, while ground-feeding birds such as towhees and thrushes favor grains. I prefer to use suet feeders when the weather is cold, to minimize the likelihood that the fat will melt or become rancid.

Add only small amounts of seed to the feeders, to ensure that the food is fresh and consumed during the day, and remove any seed on the ground by nightfall to minimize attracting rats and mice. Sadly, if rats and mice are attracted to your bird feeders, it's best to just take down the feeders. Prevent squirrels from eating the birdseed by placing

the feeder at least 6 feet off the ground and 8 feet from nearby buildings, trees, or tree branches. Add a squirrel baffle over the feeder so squirrels cannot reach it from the top. A baffle can also be placed just below the feeder, to prevent squirrels and vermin from climbing up the pole.

Birdbaths and Ponds

Add birdbaths and other water features, such as rocks with depressions that hold water, so that birds and pollinators will be inclined to stop by for a bath or drink year-round. Place birdbaths near shrubbery, trees with low branches, or brush piles to provide nearby shelter, although some birds are perfectly happy to use a birdbath in an open area. Since water is scarce during the dry summers of the Pacific Northwest, providing fresh water in the summer will definitely prompt birds to drop by your yard. Keep the water fresh by changing it every few days, particularly in the summer months, and scrub the bath with a plastic brush to remove dirt, insects, and algae as frequently as needed as determined by visible inspection.

If mosquitoes aren't on your guest list, you can prevent their larvae from hatching in warm weather by simply changing the water every 2 to 3 days. When it is not possible for you to change the water this frequently, you

TOP: *House sparrows at a bird feeder with a seed mix.*
BOTTOM: *Pine siskins on a thistle seed feeder.*

The sound of running water attracts this Wilson's warbler and yellow-rumped warbler to the fountain.

can add mosquito dunks containing the bacterium *Bacillus thuringiensis israelensis* (Bti) to the water. These are typically effective for at least 30 days and can be purchased at home improvement stores.

Another useful water feature for wildlife is a pond. A small garden pond can provide habitat for an amazing diversity of wildlife and plants. Unless you have a spring or small stream as a year-round source of water in your yard, you may wish to construct a seasonal pond that goes dry in the Northwest summer. However, you need first to decide what size and type of pond you want and what specific purpose you want it to have. To get a better idea of cost, practicality, and maintenance, I suggest you first consult a nursery that specializes in water features (see Resources).

Nest Boxes

Many cavity-nesting birds build their nests in old decaying or dead trees. In the built urban environment, most dead trees are removed because of their potential to be a safety

PETS IN THE YARD

Cats are major predators of urban birds, so keep your kitty inside, for the birds' sake as well as his or her own; cats kept indoors live longer than outdoor cats because they are protected from wild predators, dogs, traffic, and other hazards of city life. Dogs should be kept on a leash or confined to a kennel or specific area of the yard; they kill many forms of wildlife if allowed to run free.

A sweetgum snag is put to use as a support for a chickadee nest box.

a given species. Here are tips for building and placing a nesting box:

- Make sure your box is made of material that is strong, free of preservatives or toxins, and a good insulator. Western red cedar, 1 inch thick, is a good choice.
- Nest boxes require several ventilation holes in the top and drainage holes in the bottom.
- Hinge the bottom or side of the box so it can be easily examined and cleaned.
- The roof should hang over the entrance hole to keep the cavity dry and to keep predators from reaching the entrance from above.
- For added protection from raccoons and other predators, use a commercially available entry guard, or make one yourself by drilling an entry-size hole in a block of wood and mounting it in front of the entry.
- Mount the boxes at least 6 feet high to further deter predators.
- Make sure tree limbs do not block the entryway.
- Place nest boxes where they will receive morning and early afternoon sun but be shaded from the hot late afternoon sun. Face the entry toward the southeast, away from the prevailing northwest winds.
- Once the young birds permanently leave the nest, clean the nest box so it's ready for a new brood.

POLLINATORS

Pollinators are the matchmakers of the wildlife world. They play a key role in the sex lives of plants, transferring pollen from

hazard. To help attract more bird species to your yard, you can buy or build nest boxes. Different bird species require different kinds of boxes, with varying entrance diameters and positions, floor sizes, and depths, so you should first decide which species you want to attract. Check local sources such as the Audubon Society for specific requirements of

GET TO KNOW THE BIRDS

Hundreds of bird species call the Pacific Northwest home at least part of the year, and wherever you live in the area, you have the opportunity to encounter birds every day. If you listen to their calls and observe them closely you will get to know them, and they will help you connect with the beauty and wonders of nature. Their broad diversity and their propensity toward specialized habitats allow them to be excellent barometers of the health of the garden. They also play a key role in controlling unwanted insects and small mammal populations.

Because birds are vulnerable to habitat alteration, degradation, and loss, bird populations are in significant decline. Each of us can do our part to preserve the diversity of bird populations by creating sustainable landscapes that provide healthy habitats for birds and pollinators.

Many excellent regional field guides are available. For a list, see Resources.

flower to flower, plant to plant. If all goes according to plan, this results in fertilization and reproduction.

Nearly 75 percent of flowering plants rely on pollinators to set seed or fruit. Along with providing courier services, they serve as an important food source for birds, mammals, snakes, and amphibians. Without them there'd be much less fruit, vegetables, and many other plant-derived products, such as fibers, oils, spices, and medicines.

Countless species participate in plant pollination, including bees, wasps, moths, butterflies, beetles, flies, bats, and hummingbirds. Among all the animal pollinators, insects do most of the work. In return, they receive sugar from flowers' nectar and protein and fat from the pollen. Unfortunately, a number of key pollinators, especially European honey-

bees and our North American bumblebees, are in significant decline because of the loss of native plants, which provide nectar and pollen, nesting sites, and habitat. Pesticides, pathogens, the Varroa mite (which harbors harmful viruses), and climate change are also major threats.

To help reverse this decline in pollinator numbers, we need to refrain from using harmful insecticides, fungicides, and herbicides. Use pesticides sparingly, and only when no appropriate substitute is available, and only as directed on the label. Never use pesticides during the day when bees are foraging, or spray on plants when they are in flower. For more information, see the section on pesticides in Chapter 9, Sustainable Care. The decline in the social honeybees that pollinate our fruits, berries, nut trees, and

Attract a range of pollinators, like this skipper butterfly, to your garden by avoiding pesticides.

cient pollinators than honeybees, particularly for fruit trees.

This gentle bee rarely, if ever, stings. The female makes its nests underground in sandy soil or in holes in old trees, where it adds provisions of nectar and pollen and lays its eggs. Each egg chamber is closed with a mud plug, which is where the mason bee gets its name. The eggs hatch and the bee larvae eat, grow, spin a cocoon, and mature into adult bees in the nest, where they remain until spring or early summer. Female eggs are placed at the back of the tunnel and the males at the front; that way, the males come out of the nest first, and as soon as the females emerge they mate with the males. Thus the nectar- and pollen-gathering, egg-laying cycle renews itself.

Attract mason and other wild bees to your yard by setting up wild bee houses or nesting tunnels in your yard in mid-March. These bee homes can be made from paper tubes, hollow reeds, or wood trays. Alternatively, you can purchase bee houses from your local garden center or bee-supply store. For further information about DIY nest construction and other bee-related matters, see Resources.

Situate the bee house away from any bird feeders, about 6 feet off the ground, with the tubes tilting slightly downward. It should be in a location that receives morning and early afternoon sun, such as a south-facing garage, to ensure that the bees warm up sufficiently to be able to fly. Mount the nests securely against the wall so that the box will not move. Protect

vegetables makes it all the more important for gardeners to protect, enhance, and attract our wild bee populations.

Mason Bees

North America is home to about 4,000 different bee species, and one of the more common native species in the Pacific Northwest is the orchard bee, or solitary mason bee. It looks quite similar to a house fly, with its black body and a dark blue iridescent sheen, but unlike a fly it has antennae. Although it does not make honey, it is exceptionally efficient at pollination; mason bees are much more effi-

the nests from rain and wind, and cover the house with chicken wire to prevent birds from eating the nesting bees. Take down the mason bee nests no earlier than mid-May, cover them with a fine mesh or hose stocking, and store them upright in a cool, well-ventilated garage or shed (room temperature is best for developing larvae). This will prevent pests from preying on the larvae and keep other bees and wasps from using the tunnels (which can trap the early-emerging mason bees).

In October, harvest the cocoons to prevent pollen mites trapped within the tunnels from later transferring to the emerging bees.

Paper tubes can be unrolled, or wood blocks can be opened. Note that blocks with drilled holes cannot be opened, and there is no way to clean the cocoons within them.

The viable cocoons will be large and oval shaped. Those consumed by mites will be what looks like a ball of dust but is actually all pollen mites. You will also find undeveloped larvae and possibly a leafcutter bee cocoon or other inhabitants, depending upon when the nests were collected. Clean the cocoons by submerging them in a bowl of 5 percent bleach solution in lukewarm water for 5 minutes; stir gently, and rub

LEFT: *Orchard mason bee house with paper tubes* **RIGHT:** *Bee tubes and cocoons*

Providing a range of flowering plants in your garden will attract more native bees, like this sweat bee.

vided you add a small amount of water to it once a month.

The bees should be ready to emerge around mid-March. When the daytime temperature starts reaching 55°F consistently you can transfer the bees outside. To release them, put them in containers next to the nesting material, 5–6 feet off the ground in a warm location. The containers should have a small opening so the bees can crawl out after emerging on a warm day. A small wooden box with a hole in the side large enough for the bees to crawl out (and a hinged lid so you can check on the bees) works well.

them with your hand. The mud will sink and the cocoons and pollen mites float. The goal is to get rid of the mites so they cannot transfer to the bees when they emerge from the cocoon. If there are lots of pollen mites, change out the water several times to remove them all.

Transfer the cocoons to a colander, and rinse them well in lukewarm water to remove all traces of bleach. Place the rinsed cocoons on paper towels and let them dry completely. Then place your healthy cocoons in a humid container such as the specially made plastic clamshell called the HumidiBee (see Resources), which maintains an ideal humidity level for your bees of 60 to 75 percent, pro-

Other Native Bees

Other native bees that play an important role in the pollination of wildflowers and crops include the bumblebee, leafcutter bee, mining bee, and sweat bee. Bumblebees, with their distinctive black-and-yellow banding on large, fuzzy bodies, are generalists that target many different plant species and are busy pollinating flowers over large distances from early spring until fall. Like the honeybee, they carry the pollen on their hind legs.

Leafcutter bees are so named because they use cut sections of leaves, rather than mud, to create chambers within their nests. Like mason bees, they build their nests in holes in wood. They carry the pollen on their hairy bellies and are key pollinators of our native summer-flowering plants. Mining bees, with their fuzzy blond-and-orange midsections and dark abdomens, make their nests by digging holes in the ground. I commonly see them pollinating my blueberry plants. The sweat bee looks more like a small black or dark gray fly than a bee. It carries pollen on its hind legs and is a common species in the urban Pacific Northwest. Make an effort to get to know your native bees by carefully observing them and their activities.

Attracting Pollinators

You can improve the plight of native bees and other local pollinators by attracting them to your garden with a diversity of flowering plants that provide continuous accessible nectar and pollen year-round. The first step is to identify and preserve existing pollinator habitat, as discussed in Inventory Existing Plants in Chapter 2.

The next step is to add plants that will enhance habitat. Avoid purchasing plants with double or multipetaled flowers: they may lack nectar and pollen, or pollinators may have difficulty gaining access to the nectar and pollen they do have. Double flowers are flowers with extra petals, as in many of our modern roses, camellias, carnations, daisies, and impatiens. These have a mutation that turns the reproductive parts of the flower, such as the stamen (male part) or the pistil (female part) into petals. As a result, the food source or nectaries at the base of the flower are blocked and they may have no pollen, making them of little value to pollinators.

The majority of herbivorous insects have a predilection for certain species within a plant family, and they are often able to feed on nonnative plant species from that same family. Thus, some nonnatives can attract pollinators and provide nectar, pollen, and shelter for them. But make sure to avoid planting invasive plants to attract pollinators. For example, the butterfly bush, *Buddleja davidii*—a popular and widely planted nonnative ornamental shrub attractive to butterflies—is invasive and seeds profusely in both natural and disturbed areas. Instead, plant an appropriate noninvasive alternative, such as the chaste tree, *Vitex agnus-castus*. (See Chapter 9 for more on invasive plants.)

Many plants need a range of pollinators to help them reproduce, and in turn many pollinators require multiple flower species for food. The entry for each plant in Chapter 5, Ornamentals and Edibles, indicates whether it is great for pollinators and what pollinators it attracts. To keep all participants in this transaction happy, plant a wide variety of plants and wildflowers with overlapping and sequential bloom periods, so that there will be continuous flowering throughout the growing season, including the fall and late

BLOOM SUCCESSION PLANTING PLAN

Multiple kinds of flowers in natural drifts, with a wide range of colors, shapes, sizes, growth habitats, and time of bloom, will not only be pleasing to the human eye and nose, they will also attract the greatest diversity of pollinators. Strive to have at least three different flower species blooming at any one time during the growing season. Having a succession of annuals that flower throughout spring and summer further entices pollinators into the garden. Below is a season-by-season bloom succession planting plan using plants that prefer sunny conditions (full or partial sun) and are predominantly drought resistant (a hydrozone requiring minimal water once the plants are established).

PLANT NAME (FORM)	FLOWER COLOR	FLOWER FORM	POLLINATORS
SPRING			
Basket-of-gold (P) *Aurinia saxatilis*	Yellow	Parasol	Butterflies, moths
Candytuft (P) *Iberis sempervirens*	White	Parasol	Bees, butterflies, moths
Darwin's barberry (S) *Berberis darwinii*	Orange	Bowl-shaped	Hummingbirds
Lilac (S) *Syringa vulgaris*	Purple, white	Tubular	Butterflies, moths
Lithodora (P) *Lithodora diffusa*	Blue	Tubular	Hummingbirds
Mexican orange (S) *Choisya ternata*	White	Bowl-shaped	Bees
Red flowering currant (S) *Ribes sanguineum*	Pink	Tubular	Hummingbirds
Rosemary (S) *Rosmarinus officinalis*	Blue	Lipped	Bees, butterflies, moths
Strawberry tree (S) *Arbutus unedo*	White, pink	Urn-shaped	Bees, hummingbirds
Suksdorf's large camas (B) *Camassia leichtlinii* ssp. *suksdorfii*	Blue	Bowl-shaped	Hummingbirds
Western/Crimson columbine (P) *Aquilegia formosa*	Red, orange, yellow	Tubular	Hummingbirds, moths
SUMMER			
Anise hyssop (P) *Agastache* 'Tango'	Orange	Tubular	Bees, butterflies
Beardtongue (P) *Penstemon pinifolius*	Red, yellow	Tubular	Bees, butterflies, hummingbirds, moths

Abbreviations: (A)=annual; (B)=bulb; (P)=perennial; (S)=shrub; (T)=tree

Flower Forms:

Tubular: All petals fused into a tube; most common with hummingbird flowers.

Lipped: Petals partially fused into a tube that opens out into a distinct lip; common in Lamiaceae plant family, mostly bee pollinated.

Urn-shaped: All petals fused into a squat urn with outward-curving lip; typical of Ericaceae plant family.

Bowl-shaped: Basic open flowers, petals free (not fused), usually solitary or in few-flowered clusters.

Parasol: Flowers may be tubular or bowl-shaped, but clustered into flat-topped or globe-shaped umbels.

Daisy: Typical Compositae plant family inflorescence, with a central disk of apetalous flowers surrounded by petaloid ray flowers.

Yet more inspiration for a summer blooming garden: a blend of dahlias, snapdragons, fireweed, and anise hyssop

PLANT NAME (FORM)	FLOWER COLOR	FLOWER FORM	POLLINATORS
SUMMER (CONTINUED)			
California fuchsia (P) *Epilobium canum*	Red	Tubular	Hummingbirds
Cardoon (P) *Cynara cardunculus*	Orange	Parasol	Bees
Catmint (P) *Nepata faassenii*	Lavender-blue	Lipped	Bees, butterflies, moths
Echinacea (P) *Echinacea purpurea*	Purple	Daisy	Butterflies, moths
French marigold (A) *Tagetes patula*	Yellow, orange	Daisy	Bees
Indian blanket (P) *Gaillardia pulchella*	Red, yellow	Daisy	Bees, butterflies
Lavender (P) *Lavandula angustifolia*	Blue, purple, white	Lipped	Bees, butterflies, moths
Ninebark (S) *Physocarpus opulifolius* 'Diabolo'	White	Parasol	Bees
Oceanspray (S) *Holodiscus discolor*	White	Bowl-shaped	Bees, butterflies
Pot marigold (A) *Calendula officinalis*	Orange	Daisy	Bees
Southern globe thistle (P) *Echinops ritro*	Blue	Parasol	Butterflies, moths
Sunflower (A) *Helianthus annuus*	Yellow	Daisy	Bees, wasps, beetles, butterflies, flies
Wild mock orange (S) *Philadelphus lewisii*	White	Bowl-shaped	Butterflies, moths
Yarrow (P) *Achillea* 'Moonshine'	Yellow	Parasol	Bees, butterflies, moths
FALL			
Autumn crocus (B) *Colchicum autumnale*	Pink	Tubular	Bees
Bluebeard (S) *Caryopteris x clandonensis*	Blue	Parasol	Butterflies, moths

PLANT NAME (FORM)	FLOWER COLOR	FLOWER FORM	POLLINATORS
FALL (CONTINUED)			
Crocosmia (B) *Crocosmia* 'Paul's Best Yellow'	Yellow	Tubular	Hummingbirds
Cupid's dart (P) *Catananche caerulea*	Blue	Daisy	Butterflies
New York aster (P) *Symphyotrichum novi-belgii*	Purple	Daisy	Bees, butterflies
Russian sage (S) *Perovskia atriplicifolia*	Pale blue	Lipped	Bees, flies, butterflies
Showy stonecrop (P) *Hylotelephium spectabile*	Carmine	Parasol	Bees, butterflies, hummingbirds, birds
Tupa (P) *Lobelia tupa*	Red	Tubular	Bees, butterflies
WINTER			
Christmas camellia (S) *Camellia* x *vernalis* 'Yuletide'	Red	Bowl-shaped	Bees, hummingbirds
Cornelian cherry dogwood (T) *Cornus mas*	Yellow	Parasol	Bees
Indian plum (S) *Oemleria cerasiformis*	White	Bowl-shaped	Bees
Leather-leaf mahonia (S) *Mahonia* x *media* 'Charity'	Yellow	Bowl-shaped	Hummingbirds
Nepalese paper plant (S) *Daphne bholua* 'Jacqueline Postill'	Pink, white	Tubular	Hummingbirds
Salal (S) *Gaultheria shallon*	White	Urn-shaped	Bees, butterflies, hummingbirds
Snowdrop (B) *Galanthus nivalis*	White	Bowl-shaped	Bees
Witch hazel (S) *Hamamelis* x *intermedia* 'Jelena'	Copper	Bowl-shaped	Hummingbirds

Anna's hummingbird getting nectar from bee balm.

Black-eyed susan, Rudbeckia hirta, *is a great source of nectar and pollen in late summer and fall.*

winter/early spring. Do so in groupings or "natural drifts" of each species, to assist pollinators in their search for the desired flowers. A natural drift is a generous number (five, seven, nine, or more) of a single variety of plant that appears to have occurred naturally through self-seeding or other unaided means of planting, oftentimes more densely planted in the middle of the group and more widely spaced at the edges where it blends into another group planting.

Plants in the aster (Asteraceae), mustard (Brassicaceae), carrot (Apiaceae), and mint (Lamiaceae) families are usually excellent sources of pollen. For additional information, see Resources.

Pollinators are more likely to stop by your garden if within it they can find a variety of microclimates, fresh water, and pesticide-free soil for nesting, egg laying, and overwintering. Like grandparents baking cookies to entice the grandkids to come over, plant the plants that bees, birds, and bugs love, to draw them to your yard. You will not only create a rewarding garden, filled with pollinators throughout the seasons, but you will be ensuring that your landscape thrives—and that your food crops are getting what they need in order to produce the fruits and vegetables you like to eat.

CHAPTER CHECKLIST

☐ Create a home for birds and other wildlife by adding a bird feeder, nesting box, and birdbath or pond to your yard.

☐ Create a home for pollinators like native bees and hummingbirds by adding tunnel nests or bee houses, and planting natural drifts of flowers of many colors and shapes to attract them.

PART 3

GOING FURTHER

9

SUSTAINABLE CARE

Sustainable methods are those that consider the needs of future generations as well as the present one, match use of resources with availability, are in balance with nature, and do not degrade the environment. We have already covered some of these principles in earlier chapters, such as making mulch and compost from plant debris, which is then used to enrich soil and suppress weeds (Chapter 3, The Living Soil); creating multilayered landscapes with a diversity of plants, growing different vegetables in succession in the same garden area, and growing cover crops to minimize erosion and improve soil quality (Chapter 5, Ornamentals and Edibles); and encouraging wildlife and pollinators by building habitat (Chapter 8, Urban Wildlife Sanctuary). The next step is to use integrated pest management, which relies primarily on mechanical, cultural, and biological strategies rather than chemical measures to control pests.

INTEGRATED PEST MANAGEMENT

Integrated pest management (IPM) is a science-based approach to managing and monitoring plant diseases, insects, weeds, and other pests in the garden. The first step in IPM is to create garden conditions that promote plant health while also discouraging pests and minimizing pest habitat. This requires regular assessment and monitoring; often—but not always—a plant's appearance will tell you all you need to know.

OPPOSITE: *Ladybugs help control unwanted insects in the garden.*

When removing rust-affected leaves from roses, put them in the trash, not in the compost pile.

Promoting Healthy Cultural Conditions

Most plant problems are not caused by pests or pathogens. More often than not, plants become unhealthy due to inappropriate cultural conditions, such as lack of water or oxygen, nutrient imbalance, or unseasonably cold weather. When assessing a plant's health, consider uniformity versus irregularity. If you see just a couple of trouble spots here and there, pests may be the problem. But if all the leaves of a plant are uniformly affected, the trouble is more likely caused by physical or chemical factors. The following are the most common problems.

Lack of Water, or Salty Water

Leaf wilting, necrosis of leaf tips and margins (tissue death usually evident as black or brown tissue), or early leaf drop of young leaves may indicate lack of sufficient water. Plants exposed to saltwater or deicing salts can also display wilting.

Anaerobic or Compacted Soil

The same symptoms—leaf wilt, necrosis, or early leaf drop (but in this case of older leaves)—may indicate anaerobic soil conditions (lack of oxygen) because of poor drainage and/or compaction. To evaluate whether

The squash plant on the left with yellow leaves is showing nitrogen deficiency, while the potted plant on the right, in well-balanced soil, is a healthy green.

there is poor drainage and/or compaction, see Chapter 3.

Extreme Weather

Unseasonably hot weather can also contribute to wilting and necrotic lesions on the leaf surface. Unseasonably cold weather in early fall or late spring can cause freezing stress; after the frozen tissue thaws, some plants may appear flaccid and have marginal leaf browning and necrosis.

Nutrient Imbalance

The use of too much chemical fertilizer can lead to an excessive amount of soil phos-phate, which can then limit a plant's uptake of micronutrients. A deficiency in plant-available nitrogen, evident as a uniform chlorosis (yellowing) of leaf tissue in older leaves, is a relatively common occurrence in urban landscapes. When the soil is low in nitrogen the plant will have stunted growth and small light green to pale yellow leaves. In contrast, when the soil's nitrogen content is too high the plant will have rapid, lush growth with decreased flower production and poorly developed roots that are sensitive to soil pathogens; as a result, it will be top-heavy and tend to blow down in the wind. If you

LEFT: *Learn to recognize a ladybug pupa.* **RIGHT:** *Orb weaver spiders are efficient at capturing insects.*

suspect nutrient excess or deficiency, test for soil nutrients to guide corrective action (see Chapter 3).

ENLISTING NATURE'S PEST CONTROL AGENTS

Only a small percentage of garden insects are harmful, while most are beneficial. The beneficial insects and other arthropods, such as spiders, predatory mites, and daddy long-legs, prey on insects that attack plants, such as aphids, mites, thrips, and tent caterpillars. There are two types of beneficial organisms that provide pest control for the home gar-den: predators that either chew on or ingest the body liquids of their prey, and parasitic insects (parasitoids) that lay eggs on or near other insects, after which their larvae eat the host insects. These organisms are nature's pest control agents, maintaining the natural balance. It is important to get to know some of these good guys and learn to attract them to your garden.

Nearly everyone knows the predator lady beetle, or *ladybug*, which eats aphids and whose larvae feed on aphids. Other similar predators are leafhoppers, mealybugs, mites, thrips, and other soft-bodied insects. The *ground beetle* eats slugs, snails, cutworms, maggots, and caterpillars. The beautiful green *lacewing* has a voracious appetite for aphids, while its larvae eat thrips, spider mites, whiteflies, leafhoppers, scale, and other bad guys. The *damsel bug*, both adult and nymph, feeds on aphids, leafhoppers, mites, small caterpillars, spider mites, and thrips. The *hoverfly*, which resembles a wasp, is an important pollinator, and its larvae devour aphids and other soft-bodied, plant-sucking insects.

Then there are parasitic wasps such as the *trichogramma*, which looks like a tiny, black fly and eats the eggs of moths and butterflies, thus preventing caterpillars from emerging. And the *tachinid fly*, whose larvae eat cutworms, squash bugs, sow bugs, and other pests. Many of these predators and parasitic insects also feed on flower nectar and pollinate our garden plants. The best way to encourage and keep these beneficial creatures in your garden is to provide a diversity of native plants, and never use pesticides.

Two other animals, spiders and bats, play an important role in controlling pests. Spiders keep insect populations under control by consuming large numbers of them. They prevent insect pests from becoming overly dominant and destructive in our yard and vegetable garden. Spiders are also an

Both the leafhopper (left) and yellowjacket (right) have roles as predator and prey in the garden.

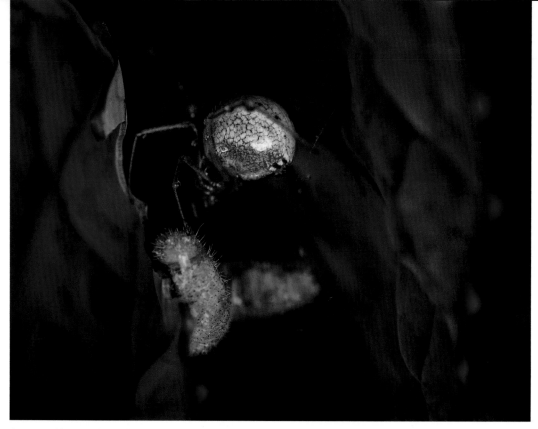

A green spider attacks a cabbage lopper caterpillar.

important food source for birds and many other animals; hummingbirds depend on spider webs for nest-building material.

Bats, like spiders, play a vital role in the health of the urban ecosystem. They eat vast amounts of night-flying insects, including harmful ones that damage crops and garden plants, along with thousands of mosquitoes. They are important pollinators of a variety of fruits and nuts, including bananas, avocados, dates, figs, peaches, mangoes, and cashews. Bats begin their daily activity at dusk after leaving their roosting sites. Near or at darkness they forage for a few hours, after which they roost again. They may forage again before return-

ing to their daytime roosting site. Preserve and protect these garden allies and their habitats by providing a pesticide-free environment with lots of insects for spiders and bats to eat.

IDENTIFYING AND MANAGING PESTS

If a pest problem is evident, first identity the plant, then identify the pest. To do so, use a magnifying glass to carefully examine the plant and the damage. Here are some signs and their causes:

- Loss of partial or whole leaves: chewing insects
- Notches along the edges of leaves or holes in leaves: weevils or grasshoppers

- Entire leaves eaten: caterpillars or cutworms
- Wilting or color change: sucking insects, which suck sap out of plant cells or inject toxic substances into the plant (for example, the lace bug can cause yellow flecking on the top of rhododendron leaves)

Unfortunately, many plant pests that cause serious damage may no longer be present when symptoms are noticed because they've already left to find target plants elsewhere; also, many, such as bacteria and viruses, are too small to be seen. If insects are present, one way to more definitively identify them is to take a piece of the plant, along with any

ENLISTING BENEFICIAL INSECTS

So how do we enlist this army of good guys for natural pest control? Many of the plants attractive to pollinators discussed in Chapter 5 and those cited in Hydrozone Planting Plan for a Perennial Border in Chapter 7, Water, along with the many plants in the Bloom Succession Planting Plan in Chapter 8, will attract these beneficials.

As many of these beneficial insects have short mouthparts, they prefer flat clusters of tiny, shallow flowers whose nectar and pollen is more readily accessible to them. To attract good insects, grow

- plants in the daisy family, such as aster, cosmos, and yarrow;
- plants in the carrot family, such as cilantro, dill, fennel, and parsley;
- plants in the mint and mustard families;
- cover crops such as buckwheat and clover;
- annuals such as sweet alyssum, cosmos, marigolds, sunflowers, and zinnia;
- perennials such as basket-of-gold, blazing star, candytuft, coreopsis, lavender, and Shasta daisy;
- herbs such as angelica, borage, catnip, and caraway.

These insectary plants should be a permanent component of Northwest gardens, including vegetable gardens. You can also let some of your vegetables, such as carrots and broccoli, flower to help attract the good insects.

Certain night-scented or late-day-blooming flowers will help bring bats to your garden by attracting night-flying moths and other insects bats like to eat. These include fleabane, goldenrod, catchfly, phlox, and evening primrose. You might also consider building bat houses if you know that bats live in your area.

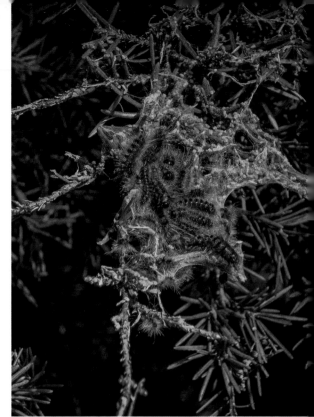

LEFT: *Caterpillars such as this cabbage lopper may eat a few plant leaves, but it is worth the trade-off. The plants will grow back and your garden will benefit from the presence of moths and butterflies.* **RIGHT:** *Even tent caterpillars, which can decimate but likely not kill deciduous trees, should be considered part of the natural balance.*

insects you find on it, to the nearest Master Gardeners clinic.

For more information, your county extension service is usually a good source. Go to www.pickyourown.org/countyextension agentoffices.htm to find your extension service. For other sources, see Resources.

Once you find the specific pest responsible for your plant damage, you'll need to decide just how much damage you—and the garden—can tolerate before taking action. Often, when you first notice a pest problem, the number of pests may be relatively low. Through visual monitoring, keep track of the pest to see if the numbers and plant damage are increasing.

Some pests, of course, may be difficult to see or count because they are only present at night or are constantly flying. For these tricky little buggers, use sticky traps or pheromone traps to monitor them. Take a wait-and-see approach: a healthy soil full of beneficial organisms and a garden full of beneficial control agents such as praying mantis, thrips predator, damsel bug, tachinid fly, mealybug destroyer, parasitic wasp, and beneficial nematode might be able to control the pests without your getting involved.

You can maximize your chances of natural biological control agents eventually handling the problem by planting multilayered landscapes with structural, functional, and species diversity, as described in Chapter 5, to attract them to the garden. Sometimes the situation will right itself, and time is the best medicine. For example, many deciduous trees can withstand considerable damage to their leaves without any serious consequences to their health. When it comes to pest control, less is always best. When to step in and act depends largely on your tolerance level. If you deduce that the plant will not recover from the pest infestation or the infestation will spread to other plants, then it would be prudent to take action.

Start with physical or cultural controls, such as picking slugs off of plant leaves, hosing aphids off with a strong spray of water, or trapping whiteflies with sticky colored tape. If those methods don't work well enough, you can deliberately import biological predators or parasites, such as the bacterium *Bacillus thuringiensis* (Bt), beneficial nematodes, or green lacewings. If, after careful study, you decide that beneficial organisms aren't going to satisfactorily handle the problem pest, learn more about your adversary, in particular its life cycle. This will help you to time your attack for when it is

Providing host plants for caterpillars in your garden is an important step in ensuring you'll have moths and butterflies, which are key pollinators.

at its most vulnerable—of course, using the least toxic chemical control available, such as insecticidal soap, horticultural oil, or careful spot spray.

Using Pesticides: The Very Last Resort

Although pesticides, particularly herbicides and insecticides, are applied extensively in urban and agricultural settings, they really should be considered a method of last resort.

We all need to understand the long term effects of pesticides on not only our food but also the soil.

Pesticides have their benefits: they've made it possible to feed a steadily growing population by keeping tired soil productive. But at this point in history, it's fairly common knowledge that overusing them poses serious threats to humans, wildlife, and the environment we all share.

The impact of pesticides varies with the type of chemical applied and the number of applications. After a onetime application, most changes in soil biodiversity are relatively short-lived. Repeated applications, however, can lead to more lasting effects. Formulations of glyphosate, such as Roundup, are currently the world's most popular and widely used herbicides in urban settings. They do a good job of killing weeds around homes and parks, but studies show that when glyphosate is released into the *rhizosphere*, an area of soil near the surface that is home to many plant roots, it helps to increase populations of certain plant pathogens like *Phytophthora*, *Fusarium*, and *Pythium*, which cause disease. This and other evidence suggests that glyphosate makes plants more vulnerable to soilborne fungal pathogens, increases detrimental manganese-oxidizing bacteria, and decreases the number of beneficial organisms such as mycorrhizae and the symbiotic nitrogen-fixing *Rhizobium* bacteria.

It's not just plants that can get sick from pesticide, herbicide, and fungicide overuse.

Over the past fifty years, pesticide-intensive farming practices have significantly damaged farmland biodiversity, including the natural enemies of pests and invertebrates. Pollinator species, particularly bees, are struggling—pesticide use has been linked to colony collapse disorder, whereby honeybees abandon their hives during winter. There is also evidence that glyphosate can kill aquatic species such as tadpoles. And a typical formulation of glyphosate (Roundup) is cytotoxic to human liver cells, at concentrations far below those used in agricultural applications. In addition, a growing concern is that weeds resistant to glyphosate are now present in the vast majority of soybean, cotton, and corn farms in some American states.

Some farmers have turned to applying several different herbicides in a single season, significantly increasing their costs while also posing new dangers to humans and the environment. The good news is that glyphosate breaks down relatively quickly, usually within days, and therefore is less likely to run off into rivers and streams. However, its residues can persist in the soil for many months.

To minimize your contribution to this problem, use pesticides only when absolutely necessary and only in the context of a well-developed integrated pest management plan. Use the least toxic pesticide, the minimal number of applications for the problem, and the appropriate formulation in the right dose; strictly follow the precautions and instructions on the pesticide label. Do your best to prevent it from drifting into water systems. Spot-spray the pesticide on targeted pests rather than broadcasting it over a large area. It is also best to spray on a dry and windless day, early in the morning when flowers are not blooming. And be sure to wear gloves.

Neonicotinoids

Among the insecticides most commonly used by both homeowners and farmers are neonicotinoids, and the form most used by homeowners is called imidacloprid. When it is used as a granular application or as a soil drench there is usually minimal contact with bees and other beneficial insects. However, residues of the pesticide can persist in the soil. The water-soluble pesticide is also widely used to treat seeds and spray ornamentals, lawns, and fruit and vegetable crops. It is taken up by plants and slowly converted to toxic breakdown products. These toxic residues persist in plant tissue for a long time and they end up in nectar and pollen. Consequently, bees and other beneficial insects consume the neonicotinoid residues. Bees exposed to sublethal amounts of these residues can exhibit numerous adverse reactions, such as reduced reproduction and problems navigating and finding food. It is also likely that bees exposed to this pesticide are more susceptible to pathogens and parasites.

To minimize the negative impact of neonicotinoids on multiple bee species, the Xerces

Society for Invertebrate Conservation recommends their use be suspended for bee-visited crops such as soybeans, cotton, corn, apples, and blueberries, and banned for cosmetic purposes on ornamental and landscape plants.

Nearly all forms of agriculture and land management require some form of pest control, and pesticides are the most widely used tool for this job. Hopefully, with the exploration of new approaches to plant protection and the development of safer products, better solutions for restoring biodiversity and maintaining agricultural productivity are right around the corner.

INVASIVE SPECIES

Invasive species are nonnative species that adversely affect a particular habitat or region, by causing or having the potential to cause environmental, economic, or human harm. Invasive plants spread rapidly, form self-sustaining populations, dominate their habitats, and damage the environment.

Nonnative species are introduced both intentionally and accidentally, through landscaping, agriculture, forestry, or shipping. Most do not become invasive, but a small fraction become serious pests in both natural and managed ecosystems and cause a wide array of environmental problems. And once an invasive species such as purple loosestrife or Japanese knotweed becomes established, it can be costly and sometimes impossible to eradicate.

Invasive species compete with natives for limited resources, and they sometimes alter the soil's physical and chemical properties to the extent that it becomes unsuitable for native trees, shrubs, and perennials, endangering the creatures that depend upon them. They can reduce biodiversity by altering the food web on a small or large scale: Once an invasive species takes over an area, the native plants that provide food and shelter for native animals die off, and then the native animals die off. Invasive species can damage both aquatic and land habitats for wildlife; block wildlife access to water, spawning grounds, and other resources; change the frequency or intensity of disturbances such as fire and flooding; and alter the water cycle.

Minimizing Invasive Species

Nature lovers and the plant-buying public can play an important role in controlling the spread of invasive species. Preventing new invasive plants from being introduced is by far the most cost-effective and efficient approach. Gardeners must be vigilant in detecting new invasions by learning to identify plants with opportunistic traits and persistently eradicating the worst invaders.

Many states have early detection and rapid response (EDRR) projects through their noxious weed programs. The Washington State Noxious Weed Control Board has a comprehensive website for locals (www.nwcb.wa.gov/), and the Center for Plant Conservation's site (www.saveplants.org/) has a

A widespread northwest invasive plant, Scotch broom, Cytisis scoparius

broad geographical reach. Both have information on identifying and curtailing noxious weeds.

The best approach to managing invasive plants is to be proactive and not allow the plant to enter a new area in the first place. On a national level, this is accomplished by enforcing quarantine laws, inspecting imports, and banning the importation and sale of plants that are likely to cause problems. Most states have a quarantine list of plants and seeds whose importation and sales are prohibited in the state. A key activity of EDRR programs is to organize and make available lists of nox-

ious weeds using a weed-risk assessment process. In Washington State, invasive weeds are placed in three categories:

- *Class A weeds* are rare, have limited distribution in the state, and are mostly newcomers, such as giant hogweed (*Heracleum mantegazzianum*) or kudzu (*Pueraria montana* var. *lobata*). All Class A weeds are on the quarantine list, and landowners are required to completely remove them.

- *Class B weeds* are widespread in some parts of the state but rare or absent in other parts, for example, Japanese knotweed (*Polygonum cuspidatum*) or Scotch broom

Allowed to climb a tree, English ivy, Hedera helix, will smother it and prevent sunlight from reaching the leaves, resulting in a loss of tree vigor. Eventually, the tree will weaken and die, and the over-weighted tree will be susceptible to falling down.

(*Cytisus scoparius*). The goal is to reduce their infestation in already infested areas and prevent their spread into new areas.

- *Class C weeds* are typically common and widespread, such as English ivy (*Hedera helix*) and Himalayan blackberry (*Rubus armeniacus*). Landowners are usually not required to control Class C weeds, except when they threaten natural resources or agriculture.

Oregon has its own classification system: *Class A weeds*, which occur in small enough numbers to make eradication or containment possible, are required to be eradicated or intensively controlled. *Class B weeds*, which are regionally abundant but may have limited distribution in some counties, are required to have intensive control on a specific case-by-case basis; when that is not feasible, biological control by deliberately importing biological predators or parasites to help control the selected invasives will be the primary control. British Columbia has three categories of noxious weeds: those noxious throughout the entire province, weeds noxious within regional districts, and other selected invasive plants.

Local weed boards can provide advice in the form of educational materials and outreach efforts to local landowners about which species are targeted for eradication or containment and how to undertake effective control measures. A successful invasive-plant management program requires a combination of approaches, including a voluntary code of conduct, best management practices, and appropriate government regulations. A workshop in 2002 on voluntary approaches for reducing the introduction and spread of invasive species in St. Louis, Missouri, came up with what the gardening public and other groups, including nursery professionals, landscape architects, botanical gardens and arboreta, and government agencies should be doing to prevent or minimize invasive species in our gardens (www.plantright.org /pdfs/StLouisDeclaration.htm). Its provisions for the gardening public include the following:

- Buy only noninvasive species when you acquire plants.
- Remove invasive species from your yard and replace them with noninvasive species suited to your site and needs.
- Do not trade with other gardeners if you know their plants are species with invasive characteristics.
- Request that nurseries promote, display, and sell only noninvasive species.
- Volunteer to help remove invasive plants in your neighborhood.

Many established invasive species continue to persist and expand their range, while new species continue to appear around us through a variety of pathways. This poses a major challenge for gardeners wanting to maintain diverse, multilayered, sustainable landscapes. You can help meet this challenge by following the gardeners' voluntary

Although dandelions can readily spread with the help of the wind, their flowers provide nectar and pollen to bees and other beneficial insects, and their young leaves are great in salads.

This garden perfectly utilizes dense, site-appropriate groundcovers and shrubs to minimize weeds.

code of conduct for dealing with invasive species.

WEEDING "WEEDS"

All unwanted or undesirable plants fall into the general and arbitrary category of "weeds." These can be invasive species, or noninvasive species that you simply want gone. Most people call a plant a weed if it upsets natural processes, is aggressive, and outcompetes its neighbors.

It's good to have some weeds, because many of them attract beneficial insects. But you'll want to keep them from getting out of hand and going to seed. Follow the principles of integrated pest management, by employing control strategies in order of least intrusive to most.

- Remove weeds before they get established and upset the harmony of the already established plant community.
- Minimize bare ground by planting dense, site-appropriate groundcovers.
- Cover bare ground or space around woody plants and perennials with organic mulch, such as wood chips with leaf mulch, to stop weedy species from germinating.

- Place mulch around new plants to stop weeds from germinating but do not add mulch directly in the planting hole, because soil that is different from the surrounding soil may cause root circling or retard plant establishment.

If physical means of managing weeds are not successful, determine whether a biological control is available. Use toxic herbicides only if less toxic control measures fail. Sometimes you will need to use a combination of measures.

CHAPTER CHECKLIST

☐ Practice integrated pest management (IPM), a science-based approach to monitoring and managing plant health and disease, insects, weeds, and other pests in the garden.

☐ Use plants that attract beneficial organisms that in turn help control nature's pests.

☐ Properly manage pests by 1) identifying your plant and pest, 2) assessing the seriousness of the damage, 3) learning the life cycle of the pest, 4) applying the least toxic control methods first.

☐ Minimize invasive species by preventing new invasive plants from being introduced and by being persistent in eradicating the worst invaders.

10

THE BROADER
ECOLOGICAL COMMUNITY

Just as you, an individual urbanite, are part of the city's larger community, urban gardens are part of a broader ecological community. No matter how small or seemingly isolated, your garden is a vital piece of the puzzle of our varied urban and rural ecosystems and the biodiversity that thrives within them.

Most animals that are integral to pollination and seed dispersal operate on a scale broader than the individual urban garden. We can manage our neighborhoods so that gardens and green spaces are coordinated, maximizing wildlife habitat and giving plants and animals places to spread, migrate, and reproduce. Strips of natural vegetation, or habitat corridors, let previously isolated populations of wildlife mingle, thus promoting genetic diversity.

These green networks connect our fragmented habitats, providing healthy environments not just for bees and birds and salmonberry, but for humans in need of fresh air and sunshine. For this reason, we must treat gardens not as independent entities but as collective and interconnected patches of habitat.

If you aren't already, there are many ways to get involved. You and your neighbors can take garden management as an opportunity to get to know one another, and collaborate and coordinate habitat zoning and the maximizing of urban biodiversity. You can also join a gar-

OPPOSITE: *Green spaces are peaceful refuges in busy urban environments.*

Mixed plantings will attract a variety of pollinators.

den club, (check The Garden Club of America's club list, www.gcamerica.org/clubs, to find a garden club in your area) or residents association. Such organizations often gather to engage in friendly activism, working with local governments on citywide regulations and financial incentives to support local wildlife conservation. From gardeners and landscapers to urban planners and developers to policymakers and ecologists, everyone has a part to play in urban biodiversity conservation.

The following sections cover several issues that you and your neighbors or garden club can learn about and get behind.

PRESERVING HABITAT AMID URBAN DEVELOPMENT

The Pacific Northwest is experiencing fast economic growth and rapid development. Increased demand for housing, coupled with a limited supply, is spurring development in the housing sector. This past year, less than a mile away from my home, a remnant forest was completely torn out of a fifteen-acre site. After all vegetation was removed, roads, sewer, and drainage lines were put in. Then the developer began to build homes at a rate of a house a week; as of this writing, about forty homes had been completed. While many of the homes already have a lawn, not a single flower, shrub, or tree has been planted on any of the lots.

And yet, new housing developments where the houses are generally close together present a golden opportunity to create wildlife-friendly, interconnected habitats. Should we stand back and do nothing when developments in our community proceed in the manner I just described?

As stewards of the environment, each of us has a responsibility to tread lightly on the earth and do what we can to take care of the environment around us. This means talking to your city and county officials and your neighbors about the importance of urban biodiversity and about how to apply sustainable landscape management practices. If you are buying a home in a new development, building a new home, planning on having a new home built, remodeling your home, or doing a garden makeover, this is your opportunity to provide an example to your neighbors and community of how to put into practice the lessons you learned in this book. How each homeowner plans, builds, and manages his or her landscape has a big impact on the region's biodiversity and ecological processes. With an eye toward the bigger picture, it is important that urban housing developments preserve whatever open space and natural areas it can, including riparian corridors and wetlands. Implementing rigorous, low-impact development regulations in cities and counties would greatly aid in preserving habitat for beneficial wildlife.

TOP: *All vegetation was removed from a native woodland to build this new housing development.* BOTTOM: *Seattle's Pollinator Pathway, a mile-long corridor of pollinator-friendly gardens, is a perfect example of how a community can work together toward a more sustainable urban landscape*

Follow these best practices when trying to preserve habitat during development:

- Fence off tree root protection zones.
- Minimize clearing of vegetation to limit erosion and compaction.
- Minimize grading and compacting of the soil.
- Reuse or recycle vegetation and soil generated during construction.
- Stockpile existing topsoil during construction so that it can be reused on site.
- Restore compacted soil by amending it with compost to a depth of 12 inches, so that after construction the site will have at least that much uncompacted soil.
- Protect restored soils from recompaction and minimize erosion and weed growth by

Protect the root zone of street trees during construction projects.

applying 3 inches of coarse organic mulch, such as wood chips, on the soil surface.
- Minimize the amount of construction and demolition materials disposed of in landfills.

PLANTING STREET TREES

In many communities, homeowners are encouraged to plant and maintain trees along the street in front of their homes. Cities are striving to maintain or increase their percentage of tree cover in spite of increasing development, and street trees are one way to accomplish this. Some cities even have an incentive program to help citizens purchase and select a tree. Take advantage of the opportunity to plant and maintain trees between the sidewalk and street in front of your home, and encourage your neighbors and community to do the same.

Street trees usually have less underground space to spread their roots because much of the soil is under the impervious sidewalk and road, which is usually not native and is highly compacted and largely impermeable to root growth. These soils also have limited water infiltration and are deficient in oxygen, organic matter, and nutrients, and they are exposed to more pollutants. When planting a tree in these locations, mix in compost to reduce compaction and improve soil fertility (see Chapter 3, The Living Soil). Sometimes it may be necessary to replace the soil with either native soil or soil mixes that mimic the texture, organic matter content, density, drainage, pH, and nutrients of native soil, while also meeting the specific cultural needs of the tree species.

Select your tree from the list of your community's approved street trees. (Just do an online search with your city's name along with "approved street tree list" to get this information, or contact your city government.) Besides matching a tree to the site requirements and your overall goals for your yard, think about how the selection contributes to tree variety. Major street-tree losses occur when just a few species are planted and all are susceptible to the same pests and diseases. It is prudent, therefore, to combine many different plant families, genera, and species in any municipal street-tree program.

If carefully selected, street trees can beautify a neighborhood for generations.

Add water to a watering bag weekly for the first couple of years during the dry season to ensure a new tree gets well established.

It is also helpful to plant different clones or cultivars of a species to increase the genetic diversity. This requires community involvement and an effective street-tree management program that keeps an up-to-date inventory of current street trees, including species and cultivars, sizes, locations, and overall health.

The quality of the canopy is important because the amount and distribution of the leaf area of these trees largely determines their ability to provide ecosystem services. Make your contribution to this canopy by planting a tree along the street in front of your home.

MAINTAINING THE URBAN FOREST

The urban forest, which provides multiple ecosystem services to our cities, encompasses all trees in the city, on both public and private land, including those in urban parks, commercial and residential areas, vacant lots, and along our urban streets. Urban trees provide significant environmental and aesthetic benefits. If we want them to live up to their potential, grow to mature canopy height, live a long life, and provide us with all their benefits, we need to select and plant them properly and provide adequate planting conditions.

Having the right tree planted in sufficient volume of good soil is the most important factor in growing healthy, long-lived urban trees. We cannot expect city or county governments to carry out this large task themselves. A combination of outreach and educational materials along with municipal incentive programs is essential for engaging homeowners, city planners, landsape designers, and businesses in improving urban tree selection, planting conditions, and care. We all need to stand up for the plight of urban trees and get involved.

To protect and expand the tree canopy in urban areas, changes in tree ordinances are needed to protect existing trees on private property as well as those on public lands and to encourage the planting of beneficial

Urban forests offer intrinsic benefits to us all.

trees on private property. For example, you can encourage your community to offer trees at a reduced price, with oversight to ensure that the ones residents select are appropriate for their intended sites. Communities would also benefit from greater collective participation of gardeners and community groups in environmental stewardship. Collectively, these approaches have a great and generally untapped potential that can allow us to conserve and restore ecological processes and landscapes, while enhancing biodiversity in our communities.

Within your neighborhood, encourage the interconnection of highly diverse plant communities containing a variety of functional groups; share with your neighbors the goal of developing invasive-resistant plant communities and restoring functional, multilayered landscapes to residential areas. Gardeners, landscapers, urban planners, policymakers, ecologists, homeowners, renters, and landlords—all residents, not just developers and politicians—must participate to successfully conserve local natural resources and restore biodiversity

WILDLIFE CORRIDORS
Habitat loss and the breaking up of habitat into smaller patches are major contributors

A mix of drought-tolerant, pollinator-friendly plants enhance a parking strip.

to the decline of biodiversity in urban areas. Your shelter belt, in the form of a multilayered landscape with a concentrated group of primarily native trees, shrubs, and groundcovers on the border of your yard (see Chapter 5, Ornamentals and Edibles), can link up with your next-door neighbor's shelter belt to create a wildlife corridor. Connected shelter belts facilitate movement of birds and other wildlife between yards; they also aid in pol-

len, seed, and animal dispersal and promote genetic interchange.

Work with your neighbors to coordinate strategies to link shelter belts. Your residents club or garden group can work to promote urban wildlife corridors, while also encouraging government regulations and financial incentives that support local wildlife corridors and conservation. Improving habitat along city streets and other transportation corridors by replacing weedy and invasive plants with a variety of site-appropriate native and nonnative, noninvasive species also greatly helps in enhancing habitat corridors, and thus bio-diversity, for wildlife in urban areas. Without these corridors, wildlife are much more likely to be killed by cars or trucks on the road, which can contribute to their becoming endangered.

EPILOGUE
A CALL TO ACTION

Humans make up just one small strand in the web of life. Our human survival—and our everyday health—depends profoundly on this web, on Earth's vast variety of life. Unfortunately, we have to face the fact that we have severely disrupted this web and threatened the continued existence of many organisms, including, ultimately, ourselves. We are not immune to extinction. And if we do so much damage that Earth can no longer support us, it will inevitably carry on without us.

If we caused this environmental destruction, though, there must be a way to undo it. Though the window to reverse the damage is quickly closing, it is not too late; the environment can regenerate itself with our help. Responsibly caring for our ecosystems is the only way for human life to carry on, in the present and for future generations. But, like all complicated endeavors, this will require a thoughtfully planned and enduring effort.

With more than half of humankind living in cities, our first steps must be developing sustainably and restoring urban biodiversity. This can only be done by dramatically changing the way we live and the way we develop and maintain our yards, neighborhoods, and cities. We must expand our concept of urban community to include the land itself and its plants, animals, soil, and water.

OPPOSITE: *Water source for wildlife in a woodland garden*

Connecting with nature can be as simple as just playing outside.

Firsthand experience with the natural world is a good place to start. Playing in the great outdoors makes anyone, both children and adults, appreciate the earth and value conservation. The most effective way to support this is to place a greater emphasis on environmental education in our schools, to ensure that these values translate into positive action as our kids grow up and take on this extraordinary challenge.

Of course, we are all part of nature and we all—gardeners and informed citizens, public administrators and civil servants, public and private companies, and scientific and academic institutions alike—need to participate in its conservation and restoration, and come together to form community initiatives that take action. Enhancing biodiversity must be the primary goal, accomplished by conserving and restoring our natural systems: by designing and developing in ways that protect and enhance healthy ecosystems, by reducing waste and the use of fossil fuels, and by making a greater effort to conserve our natural resources, including fresh water.

Pursuing conservation where people live, work, and spend leisure time is a major enterprise. As you accept this challenge, you are not only substantially contributing to your own health and well-being, but also to the health of the urban ecosystem and the future of the planet.

RESOURCES

Climate Zones

American Horticultural Society Plant Heat Zone Map: http://ahsgardening.org /gardening-resources/gardening-maps /heat-zone-map

Editors of *Sunset* magazine. *The New Western Garden Book: The Ultimate Gardening Guide.* 9th ed. Des Moines, IA: Oxmoor House, 2012. www.sunset.com/garden/climate -zones

US Department of Agriculture (USDA) Hardiness Zone Map: http://planthardiness .ars.usda.gov/PHZMWeb/

Invasive Species and Pests

Antonelli, Art, Linda Chalker-Scott, Carrie Foss, and Jenny Glass. *Diagnosing Plant Stress*. Yakima, WA: GFG Publishing, 2009.

Chalker-Scott, Linda. *Sustainable Landscapes and Gardens: Good Science—Practical Application*. Yakima, WA: GFG Publishing, 2009.

Emanuel, Robert, Linda McMahan, and Joy Jones. *Invasive Species: What Gardeners Need to Know*. EM 9035. Corvallis, OR: Oregon State University Extension Service, 2011. https://catalog.extension.oregonstate.edu /em9035

Integrated Pest Management: www.seattle.gov /util/ProIPM

Washington State Noxious Weed Control Board: www.nwcb.wa.gov/

WSU Hortsense: http://hortsense.cahnrs.wsu .edu/Home/HortsenseHome.aspx

Plants and Community Gardens

Brun, Charles A. *Drought Tolerant Landscaping for Washington State*. Home Garden Series EM087E. Washington State University Extension, 2015. http://pubs.wsu.edu /ItemDetail.aspx?ProductID=15766

Cogger, Craig, Chris Benedict, Nick Andrews, and Andy McGuire. *Cover Crops for Home Gardens West of the Cascades*. Home Garden Series fact sheet FS111E. Washington State University Extension, 2014. www.extension.wsu.edu/clark/wp-content /uploads/sites/36/2015/06/Cover-Crops -for-Home-Gardens-West-of-the-Cascades -WSU.pdf

Forkner, Lorene Edwards. *The Timber Press Guide to Vegetable Gardening in the Pacific Northwest.* Portland, OR: Timber Press, 2012.

Garden Hotline: http://gardenhotline.org

Habitat Acquisition Trust (British Columbia). *Gardening with Native Plants.* www.hat.bc.ca /attachments/HAT_Garden_Brochure_web .pdf

Habitat Network: www.yardmap.org

Iverson, Melissa. *Starting a Community Garden: A Site Assessment Guide for Communities.* 2010. www.cityfarmer.info/2011/05/20 /starting-a-community-garden-a-site -assessment-guide-for-communities

Link, Russell. *Landscaping for Wildlife in the Pacific Northwest.* Seattle, WA: University of Washington Press, 1999.

Lohr, Virginia I. *Hardy Plants for Waterwise Landscapes* (website). Washington State University. www.wsu.edu/~lohr/wcl/

Mazza, Charles P. *Site Assessment for Better Gardens and Landscapes.* Ithaca, NY: Plant and Life Sciences Publishing, 2013.

McCrate, Colin, and Brad Halm. *Food Grown Right in Your Backyard: A Beginner's Guide to Growing Crops at Home.* Seattle, WA: Skipstone, 2012.

McMahan, Linda. *Gardening with Oregon Native Plants West of the Cascades.* EC 1577. Corvallis, OR: Oregon State University Extension Service, 2008. https://catalog .extension.oregonstate.edu/EC1577

Miles, Carol, Gale Sterrett, Lyn Hesnault, Chris Benedict, and Catherine Daniels. *Home Vegetable Gardening in Washington.* Home Garden Series EM057E. Washington State University Extension, 2013. http://extension .wsu.edu/benton-franklin/wp-content /uploads/sites/27/2014/04/Home-Vegetable -Gardening-in-WA-EM057E.pdf

Native Plant Society of British Columbia: www.npsbc.ca

Native Plant Society of Oregon: www.npsoregon.org

Oregon State University Extension Service: http://extension.oregonstate.edu/gardening/

Oregon State University Extension Service. *GardenSmart Oregon: A Guide to Non-invasive Plants.* Rev. ed. Corvallis, OR: Oregon State University Extension Service, 2010. www .portlandoregon.gov/bes/article/197414

Solomon, Steve. *Growing Vegetables West of the Cascades: The Complete Guide to Organic Gardening.* Updated 6th ed. Seattle, WA: Sasquatch Books, 2013.

Stark, Eileen M. *Real Gardens Grow Natives: Design, Plant, & Enjoy a Healthy Northwest Garden.* Seattle, WA: Skipstone, 2014.

Taylor, Lisa, and the gardeners at Seattle Tilth. *Maritime Northwest Garden Guide: Planning Calendar for Year-Round Organic Gardening.* 2nd ed. Seattle, WA: Seattle Tilth, 2014.

Turnbull, Cass. *Cass Turnbull's Guide to Pruning: What, When, Where, and How to Prune for a More Beautiful Garden.* 3rd Ed. Seattle, WA: Sasquatch Books, 2012.

Washington Native Plant Society: www.wnps.org

Washington State University Extension: http://gardening.wsu.edu/

Pollinators and Birds

Audubon Society (local chapters): www.audubon.org/audubon-near-you

Bell, Brian H., and George Kennedy. *Birds of Washington State*. Auburn, WA: Lone Pine Publishing, 2006.

Burrows, Roger, and Jeff Gilligan. *Birds of Oregon*. Auburn, WA: Lone Pine Publishing, 2003.

Crown Bees (for the HumidiBee Bee Cocoon Humidfier): www.crownbees.com

Griffin, Brian L. *The Orchard Mason Bee: The Life History, Biology, Propagation, and Use of a North American Native Bee*. 2nd Ed. Oak Harbor, WA: Knox Cellars Publishing, 1999.

Hoffman Black, Scott, Brianna Borders, Candace Fallon, Eric Lee-Mäder, and Matthew Shepherd. *Gardening for Butterflies: How You Can Attract and Protect Beautiful, Beneficial Insects*. From the Xerces Society for Invertebrate Conservation. Portland, OR: Timber Press, 2016.

Hunter, Dave, and Jill Lightner. *Mason Bee Revolution: How the Hardest Working Bee Can Save the World One Backyard at a Time*. Seattle, WA: Skipstone, 2016.

Lee-Mäder, Eric, Matthew Shepherd, Mace Vaughan, and Jessica Guisse. *Tunnel Nests for Native Bees: Nest Construction and Management*. Portland, OR: The Xerces Society for Invertebrate Conservation, 2009. www.xerces.org/wp-content/uploads/2009/11/tunnel-nest-management-xerces-society.pdf

Mader, Eric, Matthew Shepherd, Mace Vaughan, Scott Hoffman Black, and Gretchen LeBuhn. *Attracting Native Pollinators: Protecting North America's Bees and Butterflies*. From the Xerces Society for Invertebrate Conservation. North Adams, MA: Storey Publishing, 2011.

Nehls, Harry, Tom Aversa, and Hal Opperman. *Birds of the Willamette Valley Region*. Olympia, WA: RW Morse Company, 2004.

Paulson, Dennis, Bob Morse, Tom Aversa, and Hal Opperman. *Birds of the Puget Sound Region—Coast to Cascades*. Rev. ed. Olympia, WA: RW Morse Company, 2016.

Royal Horticultural Society's Perfect for Pollinators lists: rhs.org.uk/perfectforpollinators

Swanson, Sarah, and Max Smith. *Must-See Birds of the Pacific Northwest: 85 Unforgettable Species, Their Fascinating Lives, and How to Find Them*. Portland, OR: Timber Press, 2013.

Xerces Society for Invertebrate Conservation fact sheets about various pollinators: www.xerces.org/fact-sheets

Repurposing Materials

Duncan, Amy, Beth Evans-Ramos, and Lisa Hilderbrand. *The Salvage Studio: Sustainable Home Comforts to Organize, Entertain, and Inspire*. Seattle, WA: Skipstone, 2008.

Levesque, Matthew. *The Revolutionary Yardscape: Ideas for Repurposing Local Materials*. Portland, OR: Timber Press, 2010.

Oregon Hazelnuts (for shells): oregonhazelnuts.org/buy-hazelnuts/hazelnut-shells

Palmisano, Joanne. *Salvage Secrets Design & Decor: Transform Your Home with Reclaimed Materials*. New York: W. W. Norton, 2014.

Peterson, Chris. *Building with Secondhand Stuff: How to Reclaim, Repurpose, Re-use & Upcycle*

Salvaged & Leftover Materials., 2nd Ed. Charleston, SC: Cool Springs Press, 2017.

Soil

Cavigelli, Michel A., Jude E. Maul, and Katalin Szlavecz. "Managing Soil Biodiversity and Ecosystem Services." In *Soil Ecology and Ecosystem Services*, edited by Wall, Bardgett, Behan-Pelletier, et al. Oxford, UK: Oxford University Press, 2012.

Compost bin designs: www.seattletilth.org /learn/resources-1/compost

Compost bin plans: www.compostbinplans .com/compost-tumbler-plans

Hostetler, Mark E. *The Green Leap: A Primer for Conserving Biodiversity in Subdivision Development*. Oakland, CA: University of California Press, 2012.

Lavelle, Patrick. "Soil as a Habitat." In *Soil Ecology and Ecosystem Services*, edited by Wall, Bardgett, Behan-Pelletier, et al. Oxford, UK: Oxford University Press, 2012.

Puget Sound Partnership. *Low Impact Development: Technical Guidance Manual for Puget Sound*. Olympia, WA: Puget Sound Partnership, 2012. www.psp.wa.gov/downloads /LID/20121221_LIDmanual_FINAL _secure.pdf

Scheyer, J. M., and K.W. Hipple. *Urban Soil Primer*. From the United States Department of Agriculture, National Resources Conservation Service, National Soil Survey Center. Lincoln, NE, 2005. www.nrcs.usda.gov/Internet/FSE _DOCUMENTS/nrcs142p2_052835.pdf

Seattle Tilth. *Seattle Composting Resource Guide*. www.seattle.gov/util/cs/groups/public /@spu/@conservation/documents/web content/spu01_001988.pdf

Soil Biology: www.soils.usda.gov/sqi/concepts /soil_biology/biology.html

Soil testing: A & L Western Agricultural Laboratories,www.al-labs-west.com

Tzoulas, Korpela, Venn, et al. "Promoting ecosystem and human health in urban areas using green infrastructure: A literature review." *Landscape and Urban Planning* 81, no. 3 (June 2007): 167–178.

Wurst, Susanne, Gerlinde B. De Deyn, and Kate Orwin. "Soil Biodiversity and Functions." In *Soil Ecology and Ecosystem Services*, edited by Wall, Bardgett, Behan-Pelletier, et al. Oxford, UK: Oxford University Press, 2012.

Sustainable Landscapes and Ecosystem Services

Cook, Thomas W., and Ann Marie M. VanDerZanden. "Retrofitting Existing Landscapes for Sustainability." In *Sustainable Landscape Management*, 61–79. Hoboken, NJ: John Wiley & Sons, 2011.

ecoPRO Certified Sustainable Landscape Professional *Guiding Principles and Best Practices*. Version 2b, August 2014. https ://ecoprocertified.files.wordpress. com/2015/02/ecopro_bestpractices -8-20141.pdf

Millennium Ecosystem Assessment. *Ecosystems and Human Well-Being: Synthesis*. Washington, DC: Island Press, 2005.

Windbreaks: http://extension.psu.edu/plants
/plasticulture/production-details/windbreaks

Trees

Chalker-Scott, Linda. "The Myth of Fragile
Roots" and "The Myth of Collapsing Root
Balls." In *The Informed Gardener*, 29–34 and
85–90. Seattle, WA: University of Washington Press, 2008.

Elmendorf, William, Henry Gerhold, and Larry
Kuhns. *Planting and After Care of Community
Trees*. University Park, PA: Pennsylvania
State University, 2008. www.extension
.psu.edu/publications/uh143

Fitzgerald, Stephen, and Paul Ries. *Selecting,
Planting, and Caring for a New Tree*. EC
1438. Corvallis, OR: Oregon State University Extension Service, 2016. https
://catalog.extension.oregonstate.edu/ec1438

Moulton, G. A., and J. King. *Fruit Handbook
for Western Washington*. EB0937. Mount
Vernon, WA: Washington State University
Extension, 2013.

Stebbins, Robert L. *Growing Tree Fruits and
Nuts in the Home Orchard*. Revised by Jeff
Olsen. EC 819. Corvallis, OR: Oregon State
University Extension Service, 2009. https
://catalog.extension.oregonstate.edu/ec819

Water and Rain Gardens

Emanuel, Robert, Derek Godwin, and Candace
Stoughton. *The Oregon Rain Garden Guide:
Landscaping for Clean Water and Healthy
Streams*. Corvallis, OR: Oregon Sea Grant,
2010. www.portlandoregon.gov/bes
/article/474026

Greater Vancouver Regional District. *Waterwise
Gardening: A Guide for British Columbia's
Lower Mainland*. www.metrovancouver.org
/services/water/WaterPublications
/WaterwiseGardening.pdf

Hinman, Curtis. *Rain Garden Handbook for
Western Washington: A Guide for Design,
Installation, and Maintenance*. Washington
State University Extension, June 2013.
https://fortress.wa.gov/ecy/publications
/documents/1310027.pdf

Ludwig, Art. *Create an Oasis with Greywater:
Integrated Design for Water Conservation:
Reuse, Rainwater Harvesting & Sustainable
Landscaping*. 6th ed. Santa Barbara, CA:
Oasis Design, 2015.

Pasztor, Zsofia, and Keri DeTore. *Design &
Build Your Own Rain Gardens for the Pacific
Northwest*. Seattle, WA: Skipstone, 2017.

San Francisco Water Power Sewer. *San Francisco Graywater Design Manual for Outdoor
Irrigation*. https://sfwater.org/modules
/showdocument.aspx?documentid=55

Seattle Tilth. *Water Smart Toolkit: Your Guide to
Creating a Water Smart Landscape*. www
.seattletilth.org/about/water-smart-toolkit

12,000 Rain Gardens in Puget Sound:
www.12000raingardens.org

Venhaus, Heather. "Sustainable Solutions:
Water Shortages." In *Designing the Sustainable Site: Integrated Design Strategies for
Small-Scale Sites and Residential Landscapes*,
161–192. Hoboken, NJ: Wiley, 2012.

ACKNOWLEDGMENTS

I wish to thank my colleagues Drs. Simona Vuletic and Gertrud Wolfbauer for their invaluable suggestions on the initial draft. I am indebted to Cynthia Riskin for her excellent and candid recommendations for improvements in the book's initial draft, and to Sigrid Asmus for her thoughtful editorial revisions on an early draft. Anna Katz's editorial review enabled the book to be more readable and accessible to the general public, and Dr. Ross Bayton made helpful suggestions on the Bloom Succession Planting Plan. I am also grateful to Kirsten Colton for her thorough developmental and editorial review of the entire book, and I particularly want to thank the staff of Mountaineers Books and Skipstone, editor Barry Foy for his probing questions and helpful suggestions, managing editor Janet Kimball for getting the book to the finish line, and editor in chief Kate Rogers, who had the foresight and willingness to take on this project. I am thankful to David E. Perry for providing the outstanding photos.

I dedicate this book to my wife, Dr. Santica Marcovina, and to all gardeners who are doing their part to improve the environment and biodiversity.

OPPOSITE: *New fronds of native sword fern,* Polystichum munitum

INDEX

OPPOSITE: *The author's ornamental Northwest garden adjacent to a native madrona and maple woodland*

ABOUT THE AUTHOR

John J. Albers is a research professor of medicine at the University of Washington. He received his BS degree in zoology from the University of Illinois at Urbana-Champaign, and his MS and PhD degrees in microbiology and immunology from the University of Illinois School of Medicine, in Chicago. He has published 377 peer-reviewed scientific articles, contributed approximately thirty book chapters and invited papers, edited two books, and served as associate editor for several scientific journals.

Dr. Albers is also an educator for the Washington State Nursery and Landscape Association (WSNLA), an ecoPRO-certified sustainable landscape professional, and a former Washington State University/Kitsap County Master Gardener. He created Albers Vista Gardens in Kitsap County, Washington. Encompassing more than four acres, Albers Vista Gardens contains approximately 1,200 different species and cultivars. For the past eight years, Albers has regularly given presentations and tours at his garden to garden clubs, master gardeners, members of the nursery and landscape industry, and the general public. His presentations focus on growing exceptional plants for Northwest gardens, and on sustainable landscape practices. He recently published the book *Gardening for Sustainability: Albers Vista Gardens of Kitsap*.

John J. Albers lives with his wife in Bremerton, Washington. For more information on Albers Vista Gardens, please see www.albersvistagardens.org, or contact Dr. Albers directly at info@albersvitagardens.org or 124 NE 31st Street, Bremerton, WA 98310-2150.

ABOUT THE PHOTOGRAPHER

David Perry's work has been featured in *Fine Gardening* many times, including six cover features. He is also a frequent contributor to *Sunset* magazine and has had his work featured in *This Old House*, *American Rose*, *Better Homes & Gardens*, *Flower, Leaf, Garden Design, Pacific Horticulture*, and *Cut Flower Quarterly*. He is co-creator of *The 50 Mile Bouquet* (St. Lynn's Press, 2012), with author, Debra Prinzing. David also lectures and teaches photography workshops around the country and in his West Seattle garden, and offers classes in photography and storytelling, currently through the Center for Urban Horticulture at University of Washington Botanic Gardens. Learn more about David at http://davidperryphoto .com and http://about.me/david.perry.

ABOUT SKIPSTONE

Skipstone is an imprint of Seattle-based nonprofit publisher Mountaineers Books. It features thematically related titles that promote a deeper connection to our natural world through sustainable practice and backyard activism. Our readers live smart, play well, and typically engage with the community around them. Skipstone guides explore healthy lifestyles and how an outdoor life relates to the well-being of our planet, as well as of our own neighborhoods. Sustainable foods and gardens; healthful living; realistic and doable conservation at home; modern aspirations for community—Skipstone tries to address such topics in ways that emphasize active living, local and grassroots practices, and a small footprint.

Our hope is that Skipstone books will inspire you to effect change without losing your sense of humor, to celebrate the freedom and generosity of a life outdoors, and to move forward with gentle leaps or breathtaking bounds.

All of our publications, as part of our 501(c)(3) nonprofit program, are made possible through the generosity of donors and through sales of more than 800 titles on outdoor recreation, sustainable lifestyle, and conservation. To donate, purchase books, or learn more, visit us online:

SKIPSTONE

www.skipstonebooks.org
www.mountaineersbooks.org

ALSO AVAILABLE